Simply
Strategic
volunteers

**_Empowering_ People
for Ministry**

TONY MORGAN
TIM STEVENS

Group
Loveland, Colorado

Simply Strategic Volunteers
Empowering People for Ministry

Credits
Senior Acquisitions Editor: Brian Proffit
Chief Creative Officer: Joani Schultz
Editor: Candace McMahan
Copy Editor: Linda Marcinkowski
Art Director: Andrea Boven Nelson
Designer: Susan Tripp
Print Production Artist: Andrea Boven Nelson
Illustrator: Dave Klug
Cover Art Director/Designer: Jeff A. Storm
Production Manager: Peggy Naylor

Unless otherwise noted, Scripture taken from the HOLY BIBLE, NEW INTERNATIONAL VERSION®. Copyright © 1973, 1978, 1984 by International Bible Society. Used by permission of Zondervan Publishing House. All rights reserved.

Scripture quotations marked (NLT) are taken from the *Holy Bible,* New Living Translation, copyright © 1996. Used by permission of Tyndale House Publishers, Inc., Wheaton, Illinois 60189. All rights reserved.

Library of Congress Cataloging-in-Publication Data
Morgan, Tony, 1968-
  Simply strategic volunteers : empowering people for ministry / by Tony Morgan and Tim Stevens.
     p. cm.
  Includes index.
  ISBN 978-0-7644-2756-5 (pbk. : alk. paper)
  1. Church management. 2. Voluntarism--Religious aspects--Christianity.
I. Stevens, Tim, 1967- II. Title.
  BV652.M67 2004
  253--dc22
                                    2004012495

16 15 14   16 15 14

Printed in the United States of America.

What others are saying about Simply Strategic Volunteers...

"The persons needed to accomplish kingdom work are available. It's a matter of identifying them, recruiting them, and empowering them for ministry. Tony Morgan and Tim Stevens provide us what we need to accomplish this important task. I commend this resource to anyone who is responsible for using volunteers in ministry."

—Maxie D. Dunnam
President, Asbury Theological Seminary

"A delightfully down-to-earth approach to mobilizing and empowering volunteers for ministry by two leaders who live what they write."

—Bill Easum
President, Easum, Bandy & Associates
Author, Beyond the Box: Innovative Churches That Work

"All too often the evangelical church has neglected the 'priesthood of believers' concept and opted for a professionalized ministerial staff to 'do it all.' This not only sets up the local church for failure when a key ministerial staff member resigns; it also neglects a powerful source of workers for building God's kingdom. Morgan and Stevens provide us with a very practical blueprint for recruiting, equipping, and retaining volunteers. It is a must for church leaders in the twenty-first century."

—Dennis D. Engbrecht, Ph.D.
Senior Vice President, Bethel College (Indiana)

"Whoever said, 'The simple things in life are often the most profound' just might have had Tony and Tim in mind. Accessible, usable, and memorable, these simple ideas will easily move from the page to your ministry. A great follow-up to their first book."

—Dave Fleming
Leadership Coach and Consultant
Author, Discovering Your Church's Future Through Dynamic Dialogue

"The spiritual maturity of a congregation is measured in 'doers' of the Word. Morgan and Stevens teach church leaders how to empower their people for practical ministry, making both leader and volunteer more like Jesus. They've written a biblically based book that is as much a devotional as it is a scaffolding to fit people into ministry."

—Dr. Joel C. Hunter
Senior Pastor, Northland—a Church Distributed
Orlando, Florida

"Volunteers are the lifeblood of the local church. The spiritual health and vitality of the local church mirror the spiritual health and vitality of the volunteer ministry. This book gives church leaders strategic ideas to create, train, and manage a volunteer ministry that will reach a community for Christ."

—Preston Mitchell
Executive Pastor, Fellowship Church
Grapevine, Texas

"Empowering our team for ministry is the key to success in churches today. Tony and Tim give basic, fundamental tips in recruiting and training strategic teams that function well together. I truly believe this book will add value to every church staff and team."

—Dr. Tom Mullins
Senior Pastor, Christ Fellowship Church
Palm Beach Gardens, Florida

"Tony Morgan and Tim Stevens have done it again! Their second *Simply Strategic* book is a wealth of information about unleashing the laity of the church to do the work of ministry. Each chapter is incredibly practical and undeniably biblical. I pray that church leaders across the world will read and implement many of their creative ideas."

—Thom S. Rainer
Dean, The Southern Baptist Theological Seminary President,
The Rainer Group Church Consulting

"Using volunteers to their fullest potential in today's church is a huge challenge for church leadership. In this book, Tony Morgan and Tim Stevens share some practical and innovative ways to recruit, train, and retain volunteers. Many staff-led churches immediately look to hire new staff to take on new ministry roles and responsibilities. Tim and Tony will show you how your current staff can be 'equippers' in your local church, creating opportunities for volunteer service that will excite your volunteers and at the same time expand your different ministry offerings. Granger Community Church has a much lower than average staff-to-attender ratio for one reason: They know how to mobilize, equip, and motivate volunteers. This book will show you how they do it."

—Todd A. Rhoades
ChurchStaffing.com

"In their *Simply Strategic* franchise, Tony Morgan and Tim Stevens have come up with the church equivalent of Miracle-Gro. Sprinkle their 'stuff' on whatever your church is trying to do, and the lushness and beauty of what grows will take your breath away."

—Leonard Sweet
Drew Theological School, George Fox University
preachingplus.com

Contents

Dedication 8

Acknowledgments 9

Foreword 11

Introduction 13

1 Don't Ask for Help 17

2 Someone Has to Clean
the Toilets 19

3 Just Chunk It 21

4 You Can Never Spike
the Ball 23

5 We All Love a Standing
Ovation 26

6 Embrace the Chaos 28

7 There's More to Worship
Than Singing 30

8 Give People T.I.M.E. 32

9 All Those in Favor,
Say "Aye" 34

10 Turf-Guarding Has No
Place in the Church 36

11 Have Your Kids Help Load
the Winnebago 39

12 Let People Observe 41

13 E-Volunteers Make
Good Servers 43

14 Teach Shoulder-Tapping   45

15 Real Leaders Lead
Volunteers 47

16 The Attraction Factor . . . 49

17 Choose Proven Leaders . . 51

18 Dispel the Myth of
the Superpastor 53

19 If You Don't Need
a Volunteer, You're
in Trouble 55

20 Build a Replacement
Mind-Set 57

21 Learn How People
Are Wired 59

22 Take the Blame and
Give the Credit 61

23 Have a Fair 63

24 You'll Never Have
Enough Staff 65

25 It's Not All About You . . . 67

26 The More the Merrier . . . 69

27 Limit Your Span
of Care 71

28 Quality Attracts
Quality 73

29 There's More to Life
Than Doing Church 75

30 Put Down Put-Downs . . . 77

31 Expect to Hear, "I'm Not
Ready to Serve." 80

32 Limit Liability 82

33 Give Volunteers Titles . . . 85

34 Be the "Love Doctor" . . . 87

35 Respect Their Time 89

36 You Can't Fix
Everyone 91

37 Creativity Doesn't
Just Happen 93

38 Never Do Ministry
Alone 96

39 Simple Policies
Simplify Life 98

40 Don't Drop the Ball . . . 100

41 The Staff Should
Serve the Servants 102

42 Use Your "Bully
Pulpit" 105

43 Seek Ability Over
Availability 107

44 Easy Access Is Crucial . . 109

45 Master the Art
of Celebration 111

46 Volunteers Are
Sinners Too 113

47 Agree to Agree 116

48 Don't Underestimate
the Soft Sell 119

49 "Good Enough" Isn't
Good Enough 121

50 Leverage the Platform
for the "Big Asks" 123

51 Measure Ministry 125

52 Help Innocent
Bystanders 127

53 It *Is* My Job 130

54 Take Care of Those Who
Take Care of You 132

55 Not All Volunteers Are
Created Equal 134

56 Eliminate the
Lone Rangers 136

57 Commission Your
Leaders 138

58 All for One and
One for All 140

59 Be a "Supermodel" 143

60 Don't Steal Talent 145

61 Admit Your
Weaknesses 147

62 Misalignment Is Bad for
Tires *and* Churches 149

63 Leave a Legacy 151

64 Legalism Isn't Legal . . . 153

65 You Grow at
the Edges 156

66 Show Them
the Ropes 158

67 Selling in the Church . . 160

68 Discover the Path
to "Yes" 163

69 Someone Must Champion
Ministry Connections . 165

70 Mentor Your
Ministry Mates 167

71 Hire Leaders,
Not Doers 169

72 Create a System for
Encouragement 171

73 It's Not a
Life Sentence 174

74 Just-in-Time Training . . 176

75 Embrace the Tough
Conversations 178

76 Give 'Em a Win 181

77 Let People Tell
Their Stories 183

78 Hire Your Volunteers . . 185

79 Preparation Is as Important
as the Event 187

80 Dare to Debrief 189

81 Let Ministry Teams
Share Their Dreams . . . 191

82 You Can't Steer
a Parked Car 193

83 Find People Who
Get Things Done 195

84 Build Teams to Climb
Mountains 197

85 Take Volunteers Along
for the Ride 199

86 Anything I Can Do,
You Can Do Better 201

87 Celebrate in Public
and in Private 204

88 Track Ministry
Connections 206

89 Sometimes You Have
to Fire Volunteers 208

90 Brand Your Ministries . . 210

91 Sometimes the
Church Messes Up 213

92 It's True...Relationships
Change Lives 215

93 Find Your Focus 217

94 Empowerment Is More Than
Delegation 219

95 Tap Painful
Experiences 221

96 Add Fun People
to the Team 223

97 Helping High-Capacity
People 225

98 Avoid the
Blame Game 227

99 Don't Give Up 229

Discussion Guide 232

Topical Index 233

About the Authors 234

Additional Resources . . . 235

**Also in the Simply
Strategic Series...** 237

Dedication

This book is for the volunteers at Granger Community Church. You have caught the vision of biblical community. You are the "engine" behind this movement. You understand that you don't just *go* to church—you *are* the church. Your ministry is touching and changing lives throughout our community. We believe to our core that there's not a greater group of committed volunteers anywhere on the planet, and it is you who have inspired us to write this book. We know that your story will influence pastors and church leaders throughout the world. We are honored to be taking our next step toward Christ together with you.

—Tony Morgan and Tim Stevens
Granger, Indiana

Acknowledgments

To my best friend and wife, Emily. You are a constant encouragement, and I cherish your love and support. Thank you for serving Jesus beside me on this project and throughout life.

To Kayla, Jacob, and Abby. You make me smile, and I am so proud of you. You are an incredible gift from God. I treasure every day we get to spend together.

—Tony

To Grandview Park Baptist Church in Des Moines, my home church during my growing-up years. Thank you for teaching me the value and joy of serving Jesus as a volunteer.

To my lover and friend, Faith. Even after fourteen years of marriage, you still make my heart beat fast! There's no place I'd rather be than with you.

And to Heather, Megan, Hunter, and Taylor. You are so precious to me. I love you more than you can know, and I pray every day that God will give you the wisdom to know what's right and the courage to do what's right.

—Tim

To Thom and Joani and the entire team at Group Publishing. We value our partnership and are grateful for your vision to equip church leaders. Thank you for letting us do this again. Candace McMahan, thank you for helping us improve our message. You are "simply" the best.

To Joby Anders, Brian Davis, Renee Ellsworth, Steve Jones, Ron Keener, Dena McGoldrick, Patrick McGoldrick, Mark Meyer, Todd Rhoades, Greg Whiting, and Brent Wood. Thank you for reviewing the manuscript and offering suggestions for improvements. You have helped shape this book as well as our ministries.

To our assistants, Jami Ruth and Kristin Davis. We value your passion for excellence and your willingness to serve. You make us better leaders.

To our "first team"—Mark Beeson, Karen Schuelke, Mark Waltz, and Rob Wegner—and the rest of our friends and teammates at Granger. Ministry wouldn't be nearly as fun anywhere else. We love serving Jesus beside you.

And most of all, to the One who offers us new life, forgiveness, hope, wisdom, peace, and the greatest mission ever. Thank you for continuing to build your church. You are the model of servant leadership, and we are honored to follow your lead.

—Tony and Tim

Foreword

Jesus Is Building His Church

Your vision is compelling. Your call is clear. Your leadership is inspiring people to step up and serve Christ. People in your local church are going to respond. Are you ready?

What would you do if you walked into your office next Monday morning and discovered one hundred people lined up to see you? What if every one of them came to you inspired, eager, and ready to volunteer in the church? How would you react? Got a plan? Ask yourself,

- Do I have a process in place to identify each volunteer's SHAPE (Rick Warren's acronym for spiritual gifts, heart, abilities, personality, and experiences)?
- Am I ready for volunteers who come with their own agendas? Can I help them square their agendas with the mission of the church? Do I know when and how to redirect them?
- Are the opportunities for our volunteers clearly articulated? Do our people know precisely how their service, time, and efforts can be maximized for the mission of the church?
- What will I do if someone wants to do something our church doesn't believe in? How do I handle that person—and resolve the conflict that is sure to follow?
- What do people have to believe in order to serve in our church? Am I clear on the metrics required for each ministry effort? May non-Christians sing in our choir? May they sing solos? May they play piano? Must people confess Christ and be baptized before they teach our children or teenagers? Must people be members of our local church before they teach Bible studies to our congregation?

- Who sanctions and blesses each volunteer? What rewards are given for service? How are volunteers recognized, celebrated, and affirmed in our church?
- Who is responsible for the training and motivation of each volunteer? Is that the job of the pastor? Is that the responsibility of each volunteer's supervisor? Do all the leaders know what is expected of them as they direct and facilitate each volunteer on their teams?
- What enables new ministry in our church? How do we ramp up volunteers for new initiatives? Who casts that vision?
- How important is talent? What about the volunteer's ability, commitment to Jesus, or tenure in our local church? Can newcomers help? Is a level of spiritual maturity required; if so, how is that maturity quantified, and by whom?

In *Simply Strategic Volunteers*, Tony Morgan and Tim Stevens offer their brilliant thoughts on successful volunteer ministry in the local church. Their ideas are simply profound.

Tony and Tim teach you to identify, recruit, motivate, and train volunteers. They show you how to develop a team of thriving volunteers who love serving. This clear, helpful book will take your volunteer ministry to a new level.

I know these guys. I work with them. I have seen these simple strategies work in our local church. In *Simply Strategic Volunteers,* Tony and Tim give you the proven practices we have employed at Granger Community Church. These strategies have enabled thousands of volunteers at Granger to serve Christ well, experiencing the joy of team camaraderie, mutual support, and authentic community.

If you want your faithful volunteers to be fulfilled in their ministry and fruitful for Christ...

If you want the unpaid servants of Christ in your local church to thrive and soar...

If you need a clear, well-written and easy-to-read guide to help you...

...then *Simply Strategic Volunteers* is the book for you.

Mark Beeson, Senior Pastor
Granger Community Church
Granger, Indiana

Introduction

Volunteering in the local church.

Is there any other role that could be as fulfilling?

Is there any profession in which an individual could make a bigger difference than as a volunteer in the local church?

Could people possibly feel more significant than when they are worshipping Jesus through acts of service?

You know the feeling, don't you? Even if you are now paid as a staff member or pastor in a local church, you probably remember the fulfillment you felt as a volunteer. You recall the long hours—and unexplainable joy—that went with this experience.

As leaders, we work with volunteers who have made huge sacrifices to be on our team. They already have "normal" jobs. Some of them stand at the assembly line in a factory every day, ten hours a day, five or six days a week. By the time the week is over, they are wiped out. But the assembly line doesn't make them soar; it's not what they live for. No, they live for Saturday afternoons when they arrive at the church to begin sorting the bulletins for the evening service. They live to be with and pray with their team, to greet the guests as they arrive, to help new-comers who seem a little disoriented. That's what gives them a sense of purpose; it's what makes their hearts beat fast!

Others are managers and business owners and stockbrokers and firefighters and homemakers. Day after day they work their tails off to provide a service to the community and do their best for very little thanks. They try to make a difference in the workplace, they try to be a positive influence, but very few of them are fortunate enough to derive deep and abiding satisfaction from their jobs.

Even though they're exhausted, they arrive at church on a Tuesday night to begin setting the lights for the next weekend's service.

Or perhaps they lead a small group of high school students on Friday night. Or maybe they join their landscaping team at the church on Saturday morning. And strangely, after a few minutes spent serving with their team, they begin to feel better. They realize, "This is what I was made to do!"

They are volunteers in a local church. They have discovered what followers of Christ have known for centuries—that the local church is the hope of the world and it is a privilege to serve the cause of Christ as a volunteer!

It's the reason we don't hesitate to ask people to volunteer. In fact, we encourage every person who attends our church to jump in and find a ministry. It is a privilege to invite people into what might be the only activity in their lives that causes them to feel worth and significance, one in which they might experience for the first time being used by God almighty to touch another human life. We can look into their eyes with confidence and call for a commitment to service because we know that if they say yes their lives will never be the same!

It is with this confidence and passion that we wrote this book. If a church is going to sustain growth for the long haul, it's because its people understand how God has wired them to serve in areas they're passionate about. In these churches, volunteers are supported through relationships and systems, and there is a culture of celebration and excitement in the serving community. It is *the church* at its very best!

Types of Readers

People who read this book will probably fall into one of these categories:

Paid Staff—You are an "equipper." The Bible says that our job as pastors (and may we insert "church staff members") is to equip the saints for the works of service. As you read this book, ask God to help you do better. We can all do better at supporting our volunteers. We can do better with training. We can do better with celebrating their successes. We can do better with casting vision and calling the best out of a new volunteer. This book is about helping you *do better* with and for your volunteers.

Volunteer Leader—You served faithfully as a volunteer for a time, and now you have grown into a volunteer leadership position.

Someone on the church staff sees potential in you, and so you've been asked to step up and lead. This is very likely a new adventure for you. Perhaps you've led at your workplace, but it's very different leading people when you have their paycheck as leverage. Now people will only follow you if they want to. So you are on a steep learning curve. Read this book, take notes, talk to veteran leaders, and you'll do great. Always have a teachable and humble spirit.

One more piece of advice: Don't strive to be on the church staff. In some ways, joining the staff is a demotion. Just enjoy serving God without expecting anything in return, and watch how he blesses that kind of spirit.

Volunteer—You are serving on a team for your church and your God. Way to go! This book will help you find your niche, encourage the others on your team, grow in responsibility, learn how to recruit others onto your team, and deal with problems. Stay faithful so you won't become a burden to those who are leading.

Jump In!

Just jump in and start learning. If you are a *sequential* learner, start with Chapter 1 and work your way through. If you are a *topical* learner, use the topical index at the back and work your way through the areas that hold the greatest interest for you. If you're an *emotional* learner, rip out the pages you don't like so you end up with a book that contains only the chapters you like! Do whatever works for you.

If you are a *relational* learner, buy extra copies and take your group on a journey with you. Sometimes the best learning experiences occur in group settings with people you know and love. Group study is especially helpful if you lead a church and want to see your culture shift. Bring other leaders along the path of learning with you, and your attempts at implementing change won't be so painful and bloody. (We speak from experience!)

However you are wired, keep learning! Whether you are eighteen or eighty-eight, stay on a journey of lifelong learning so we can all figure out better and better ways to do this thing we call church. And never forget, the church is the hope of the world!

Don't Ask for Help

This may sound counterintuitive, but we don't ask for help at Granger. You won't see a bulletin ad indicating a *need* for volunteers. You won't hear one of the pastors talk about the shortage of workers in the children's area. You won't see "help wanted" signs posted on church bulletin boards.

Now, to set your mind at ease, this isn't because we've found the magic formula for recruiting volunteers to fill every single role that could ever exist in our ministry. We can always use more volunteers.

We don't *need* volunteers and we don't ask for *help* because we've learned that most people will not jump onto a sinking ship. When you beg for volunteer help, you might be admitting, "I have no compelling vision for this area of our ministry, and, therefore, no one willingly serves. So I'm going to try to guilt you into helping out."

> Most people will not jump onto a sinking ship.

Of course there are some people in your church who *will* respond to your plea for volunteers. Understanding that ministry sometimes involves sacrifice, they'll serve in order to keep the ship from sinking. But when people end up serving in a ministry that isn't in line with their gifts and passions, they will likely become frustrated and burned out. Then you will have created a vicious cycle: a ministry with no compelling vision and a bunch of people who'd rather not be serving in it. Oh, boy! Where can I sign up for *that* ministry team?

Instead of telling people what you need, tell them how you can help them use their gifts and experiences. Explain how they can find purpose and fulfillment. Communicate the mission and vision of the ministry, and then tell them how they could influence the lives of others by filling a particular role. Share stories about people who are already serving, and let them explain why they love to give their time and talents to the cause. Better yet, share stories about people who have benefited directly from the ministry.

We still post volunteer openings in our bulletins. Instead of asking for help, however, we offer opportunities for people to contribute to the lives of others. The focus isn't on the ministry role; it's on the person who's interested in finding a ministry. The emphasis isn't on the service that needs to be performed; it's on the people whose lives are affected by the servant.

—Tony

2

Someone Has to Clean the Toilets

Who has the gift of toilet cleaning? the picking-up-trash gift? the gift of cleaning up after a child has spewed his morning breakfast all over the floor? I'm not sure anyone has those gifts. Nevertheless, they are jobs that must be done.

Around Granger, we say that 80 percent of people's time should be spent doing what God has created them to do. If they were created to invest their lives in high school students, they should spend most of their time doing that. If they get the greatest fulfillment from planting flowers or pruning trees, they should spend 80 percent of their time working on the grounds.

> Eighty percent of people's time should be spent doing what God has created them to do.

The remaining 20 percent of their time should be spent fulfilling "roles." I may not have the gift of picking up trash, but as a Christ-follower and a member of Granger, it is my *role* to pick up trash when I see it. I may not have the gift of cleaning a room or setting up chairs or putting tables away, but many times it is my *role* to do these things to serve my church and my God.

When I was fifteen years old, I was a volunteer in the kindergarten class at my church in Des Moines, Iowa. I played the piano, spent time with the kids, and sometimes taught the lesson. One particular Sunday, Mrs. Mills was teaching the kids about responsibility and character. Without my knowing, she had observed me earlier in the hallway as I had stopped to pick up a piece of trash from the floor. She used this to begin a discussion about doing the right thing even when it's not "your job" and even when you haven't been asked to do it.

Most of those kindergartners are now married and enjoying parenthood, but it is still a good lesson for adults. The fact that Mrs. Mills noticed my good deed (which was probably more of a fluke than a pattern or lifestyle) burned forever in my mind the importance of being faithful in the little things.

Talk about this 80/20 principle with your team. Work together to figure out the "80 percent zone" in which you should each be spending your time. But also acknowledge the "20 percent zone," and celebrate when you see someone fulfilling a *role* that isn't very fun but needs to be done.

Or live with dirty toilets. It's up to you.

—Tim

Just Chunk It

One reason it's difficult to get people to commit to ministry is that we make things too big and too complex. People love simplicity. It's why you're reading *Simply Strategic Volunteers*. We've broken up everything we've learned about empowering volunteers into ninety-nine bite-sized chunks for you to digest.

Tim and I are simple guys. We lead simple lives in Granger, Indiana. And, believe me, you can't find a more appropriate place to live a simple life than Granger, Indiana.

> **People are unlikely to step into ministry roles that seem too big or too complex.**

Though sometimes Tim and I would like to believe we're extraordinary guys (especially when our wives are around), the truth is, we're quite ordinary. We drive simple cars. We live in simple homes. We write simple books. We also believe we're not the only people who like simplicity. We believe there are lots of other Hoosiers who shuck their corn just as Tim and I do...one ear at a time.

The same holds true for most people. They are unlikely to step into ministry roles that seem too big or too complex. When a responsibility appears overwhelming or impossible to accomplish alone, people will avoid it.

This is one of the reasons I love our church so much. We make ministry simple. Take children's ministry as an example. One person doesn't do it all. People serve in roles such as selecting curricula, preparing art projects, checking in children, leading worship, teaching, caring for small groups, cleaning toys, running audio and video equipment, and buying snack foods. If you asked one person to join your children's ministry in order to perform all these roles, it would be difficult to find a volunteer. We need to consider all of our ministries and decide whether "chunking" the roles might make it easier for more people to serve.

Tom Peters and Bob Waterman were the first ones to refer to this concept of chunking in their leadership classic *In Search of Excellence*. In their words, *chunking* "simply means breaking things up to facilitate organizational fluidity and to encourage action."[1]

Chunking has several benefits:

- It gets more people involved. Divide one complex role into multiple simpler roles. This way, rather than having one person work alone, you'll create opportunities for several people to work as a team to accomplish the same results.
- It creates unique positions for people with special gifts and passions. I may not be able to teach, but I love kids and I'm good with computers, so there's still a place for me to serve. For example, I could create and operate PowerPoint for the classroom teacher, I could create media to help supplement the Bible lessons, or I could develop a technology solution to automate the checking-in process.
- In most cases, chunking reduces the time commitment required of volunteers since one person doesn't have to do it all.
- It allows volunteers to improve their skills in a focused area, which increases the overall effectiveness of your ministry.

You may actually need to create *more* ministry roles if you have a shortage of volunteers. Chunk the roles so there are more opportunities for people with a variety of gifts and passions. Make the complex roles simple. You'll find yourself accomplishing more ministry, and you'll probably free up time to shuck more corn.

—Tony

ENDNOTE

1. Thomas J. Peters and Robert H. Waterman Jr., *In Search of Excellence* (New York: Warner Books, 1982), 126.

You Can Never Spike the Ball

At some time in your life, you've probably dreamed about making a winning touchdown and spiking the ball in the end zone. However, in ministry you can never spike the ball because the game is never over. Here's some more bad news:

If you are a volunteer leader,
- you'll probably never have enough volunteers,
- you'll probably never have enough money budgeted for your ministry area, and
- you'll probably never have enough space to do what you need to do.

If you are a pastor or church staff member,
- you'll probably never accomplish everything on your to-do list;
- you'll probably never feel that you have enough volunteers, staff, or money to get the job done; and
- you'll probably never feel that there's enough time to accomplish everything that needs to be done.

Why are these statements true? Consider our mission: We are supposed to win the entire world to Jesus, teaching people how to worship, developing them into fully devoted followers of Christ, engaging them in meaningful ministry, and helping them discover their life mission so they can have an impact on the world. Even if we narrow our focus from the "entire world" to our community or region, will we ever cross the finish line? Will we ever go home thinking, "Ah, I'm done now"?

If we do feel that we have enough volunteers, money, staff, space, and time to accomplish everything, then what does that say about our vision? Have we reduced our goals and dreams and made them relative to the other churches in our community rather than comparing them to God's ideal? Do we pat ourselves on the back too soon just because we are getting a lot of attention or we are doing better than others?

Tony and I were talking recently about the realities of staffing and budgets. I told him that when I first came to Granger in 1993, our weekly budget was about $7,000. I remember visiting a church at that time whose budget was over $70,000 a week. Ignorantly I thought, "When we have that much money at our disposal, we'll be able to hire the people we need and fund the ministry to which God has called us." Now that our budget exceeds that figure, I realize that I was living in a dream world.

One of the most painful aspects of my job is not being able to fund all of the important ministries or to staff all of the vital positions we've identified. Just this week we cut over $500,000 from budget requests and declined to fill forty positions. And these were all bare-bones requests without "fluff." It was all good stuff that would have deepened our ministry effectiveness.

So where is the good news? What are the lessons to be learned? Here's some help and encouragement:

> If we feel that we have enough volunteers, money, staff, space, and time to accomplish everything, then what does that say about our vision?

1. You're not alone. Every church in your community, if it is growing and seeking to serve God's purposes, is in the same boat. These churches are on the same team with us and have the same objective.

2. Trust God. How many of us would be on our knees as often if we had everything we needed?

3. You aren't a failure. Even if you've followed every strategy in this book for recruiting, placing, affirming, and leading volunteers, you probably still won't have enough volunteers. Remember, we have a *world* to reach.

4. Prioritizing is a good practice. When we don't have what we need, we are forced to prioritize. What are we doing that yields the highest return in terms of changed lives? What are we doing that isn't critical to our mission?

5. Take a deep breath. The success of God's plan to redeem the world does not completely rest on your shoulders. It is true that your mission is critical, but sometimes you need to step back, take a deep breath, verbalize to God that you still trust his plan and his timing, and ask him for a peace that is beyond understanding and a wisdom that is supernatural.

So don't be depressed. Be encouraged. We may not be able to spike the ball until we get to heaven, but we can sure make some progress down the field. Sometimes just accepting reality will give you the strength you need to make it through another intense ministry season.

—Tim

We All Love a Standing Ovation

"A person's words can be life-giving water"
(PROVERBS 18:4a, NEW LIVING TRANSLATION).

Some transitions in life are harder than others. For kids, the challenges can seem especially daunting. First they have to learn to walk. Then they have to be potty trained. They have to learn to sleep without a pacifier. Their lives become even more demanding when competitive tendencies kick in. Then kids not only have to conquer the transitions but they also feel they're competing with the other kids to grow up and move on to the next phases of life.

My wife, Emily, and I observed this recently. For many weeks, our son, Jacob, tried to make the transition that would allow him to ride his bicycle without training wheels. This made for a grueling summer, literally involving blood, sweat, and tears. And it was hard on Jacob as well.

We spent many hours running beside him, holding the back of the bike seat. You've probably experienced the drill. You run, run, run, and then you have to work up enough courage to release your child, knowing he's going to crash many, many times before he finally figures it out.

Then one evening in early fall, we decided to take a family walk around our neighborhood. Jacob jumped on his bike and asked for one more running start. We tried this several times, and each time he failed to keep the bike upright after we let go. After about a dozen failed attempts, Emily grabbed the back of the bike for another running launch. This time Jacob was determined to do it on his own, and so, declining his mom's assistance, he said, "Just cheer for me, Mommy."

Then he took off on his own and kept on pedaling all the way home—to the cheers of his mom and the rest of the family.

Like Jacob, we aren't always looking for a push. Instead, we just want someone to cheer for us. We all need cheerleaders. We all need people who will encourage us to do the next right thing. From time to time, we all need standing ovations. We need others to affirm that we're moving in the right direction and that they recognize the value of our contributions.

> We all need cheerleaders. We all need people who will encourage us to do the next right thing.

In the church, we give praise to God, but we tend to be uneasy about praising others. This is unfortunate because I believe God created us with a need to hear "well done" from time to time. It's probably why God instructs us to "love each other with genuine affection, and take delight in honoring each other" (Romans 12:10, NLT). God wants us to encourage each other because he knows that affirmation breathes life into each of us.

So the next time you catch a soloist, a teacher, a children's worker, or an usher knocking the ball out of the park, don't hesitate to stand up and cheer. It may be just the encouragement this faithful servant needs to stay the course.

—Tony

Embrace
the Chaos

As I write, I'm sitting in the home of my friends Dean and Sherri. They graciously allow me to write in their quiet, distraction-free home. I've written many chapters sitting at their kitchen table.

Their home is very different from mine. Here, everything is in its place. There are no piles of misplaced items. The countertops are spotless; the furniture is in place; the pictures and decorations have been carefully chosen and kept clean of dust and fingerprints. Situated on the coffee table are a newspaper, a book, and a pair of glasses. That's it.

My home is the antithesis of Dean and Sherri's. Every room bears recent evidence of a child's presence. The furniture is out of place because it has been run into at full speed. Immediately after being cleaned, every imaginable surface is smudged with fingerprints. For every game or craft project that is put away, it seems as if two more are started. Toys litter the driveway; in fact, I can't remember the last time I drove into the garage without first having to get out of the car to remove an obstacle.

At Dean and Sherri's house, I stop to listen. What is it that I hear? It is *nothing*. The absence of noise. I love that sound. It is the sound of peace. It is the sound of freedom from chaos.

At my house, I hear the piano. I hear a child crying. I hear an argument going on downstairs. I hear the dog. I tell myself the dog is optional. Get rid of the dog. But then I remember that I don't have the power to make such a decision in my own home. I wonder why. I begin to sulk… (Sorry, I digress.) I hear the television. I hear the electronic games. I hear someone turning on the water in the garage *again* in order to make mud out of perfectly good dirt. I hear a child asking how to get toothpaste out of hair. I hear a glass break in the kitchen and then the screams of the child who ran in barefooted to see what happened.

Why is the environment at my house so different from Dean and

Sherri's? Little people. Kids. Four of them who live with me and ten thousand of their friends who visit often.

I'll be honest. There are many days that I've longed for the peace and serenity that come with an empty nest. I've dreamed about walking through the hallway without tripping on a toy. I've fantasized about a garage that stays clean and clutter-free for more than a few minutes.

It doesn't take me long, though, to chastise myself. With the chaos of my home come life, laughter, and energy. With the chaos come indescribable love and precious moments that I want to capture forever. I want to cherish the times I lie beside Heather at night, talking about school and life. I don't want to forget that Megan will get up from whatever she is doing every time I walk in the door, to give me a hug. I don't want to lose the feeling I have when I'm laughing with Hunter after he's cracked a hilarious joke, or when Taylor says something so adult-sounding that I could swear he isn't a two-year-old.

> If you wish too much for the serenity of silence and chaos-free living, you may get what you want.

I choose to embrace the chaos. I realize that the chaos will end soon enough. Someday I'll have colleges to visit, weddings to pay for, and grandkids to play with. But I'll have the chaos of this moment for only a short while. And then the house will grow silent. Way too silent.

If you're in a church that is passionate about its mission and serious about growth, then you will regularly experience chaos. Chaos in a church can sometimes be the result of bad management or a weak leader. Often, though, it is just the result of doing everything right. It can be the result of reaching unredeemed people with the love of Christ...and then helping them grow in their faith.

I'll let you in on a little secret. When lay people aren't around, we pastors sometimes say, "If it weren't for people, church would be easy!" Sometimes working with volunteers can be chaotic. They have their own ideas, schedules, levels of commitment, piles of baggage from their past, styles of relating, opinions, and idiosyncrasies. Working with them can be very chaotic.

But let me encourage you to embrace the chaos. If you wish too much for the serenity of silence and chaos-free living, you may get what you want. And then you'll find yourself in a dying church, the sole purpose of which is preservation rather than transformation.

—Tim

There's More to Worship Than Singing

"So then, my brothers, because of God's great mercy to us I appeal to
you: Offer yourselves as a living sacrifice to God, dedicated to his service
and pleasing to him. This is the true worship that you should offer"
(ROMANS 12:1, TODAY'S ENGLISH VERSION).

As someone who can't sing a lick, I've found this passage in
Romans to be very freeing. It's reassuring to know that,
although I'll never sing a solo or lead worship at one of our weekend
services, I can still lead people in a significant act of worship by helping people serve Jesus.

In fact, the word *worship* in Romans 12:1 is translated from the
Greek word *latreia*, which means "divine service." So when Paul urges
us to experience true worship, he isn't suggesting we sing a song of
praise. He isn't encouraging us to attend a worship service to hear
someone preach from God's Word. Instead, he's calling us to serve or
minister to others.

That's why Paul is suggesting that we offer ourselves as a living sacrifice. The sacrifice he's looking for isn't limited to the use of our vocal
cords. God wants all of us. Earlier in Romans, Paul explains this in more
detail: "Give yourselves completely to God since you have been given
new life. And use your whole body as a tool to do what is right for the
glory of God" (Romans 6:13b, NLT).

Part of our role as leaders in the church, then, is to help people
understand true worship. Though I enjoy participating with others in a
service filled with teaching, prayer, and singing, which are certainly
part of worship, these elements are not *all* of worship. God wants us to

fully surrender our lives to his service. We're supposed to do *everything* for the glory of God (1 Corinthians 10:31).

That's a whole new perspective for most people who walk through the doors of your church, but it shouldn't discourage you. People are looking for real purpose in their lives. They want their lives to count beyond Sunday morning. They want to positively influence their families, their workplaces, and their communities. By helping people understand true worship and by helping them take steps toward offering themselves as living sacrifices, you will be fulfilling one of their deepest desires.

True worship through service helps to fulfill our need for significance, but it's certainly not worship's primary purpose. More than anything, worship is about pleasing God. God is pleased when we serve. Anytime you're fully committed to another person, you search for ways to express your love. God has fully revealed his heart. He's saying, "If you want to please me, give your life to me. Everything you do and everywhere you go, serve me by serving others." That's true worship. That's why it's so important for leaders in the church to see that their role is not only to impart wisdom from God's Word, but also to encourage people to take an active role in serving the living God.

—Tony

Give People T.I.M.E.

About once a month, Brian and I used to have the same conversation. As the leader of our children's ministry, he would be having difficulties with a volunteer leader. Perhaps the volunteer was being stubborn, reflecting a bad attitude, or creating other difficulties. We'd discuss our options. Most often I would end up saying, "Brian, he just needs your *touch*. He needs your *inspiration* and your *motivation*. And he needs your *encouragement*." I said this so often that one day we realized that I'd inadvertently created an acronym: T.I.M.E. So from then on, we would remind each other, "They need our T.I.M.E.!" And nine times out of ten, giving that leader our T.I.M.E. would make the tension go away.

T Is for Touch

You don't have to be a scientist to know that being touched by the right person, at the right time, and in the right way feels awfully good. We've all heard about scientific studies proving that human touch can actually improve mental and physical health, boost career performance, and even increase longevity. An appropriate touch can go a long way toward communicating love and acceptance. The well-timed touch on the arm, pat on the hand, squeeze of a shoulder, or platonic hug can improve a person's outlook, and it may be the only pure touch he or she receives.

I Is for Inspiration

We all need inspiration. We need to know why we are toiling and sweating and sometimes putting up with difficult situations or people. Make sure that your volunteers are attending the services each week.

In the rare instances that our volunteers can't attend a service because of their roles, we make sure that they receive a free CD of the service.

M Is for Motivation

Two sources can be used to motivate most volunteers. The first is training that is specific to their roles. If you can find the best seminar, workshop, book, or tape that will help them do better in their roles, most people will be very grateful. The second is stories of life change. Make sure they are hearing about the lives that are being positively influenced by their ministries. This could be done through a simple Internet-based "bulletin board" that captures and shares the stories.

E Is for Encouragement

What is the best way to encourage people? Listen. Take time to find out about their families, hobbies, and interests, and, in the process, listen to their hearts. More than anything else you can do, listening causes people to feel special and valued. Think about it: People will sit in a bar late at night, click into an online chat room, or call a nighttime radio talk show just to be heard. We all need someone who will listen to us. Of course, in order to adequately listen, you must make sure you don't have too many "direct reports" (see Chapter 27, "Limit Your Span of Care").

Make sure you are giving your people T.I.M.E. Teach your leaders the importance of giving T.I.M.E. to those under their care. If this isn't natural for you, then systematize the practice into your life. There's nothing wrong with putting it on your schedule or to-do list. People matter too much not to make this a priority.

—Tim

All Those in Favor, Say "Aye"

> "Obey your spiritual leaders and do what they say. Their work is to
> watch over your souls, and they know they are accountable to God.
> Give them reason to do this joyfully and not with sorrow. That
> would certainly not be for your benefit"
> *(HEBREWS 13:17, NLT).*

Since I accepted Christ into my life, I've been connected
to at least a half-dozen churches. In my role with
WiredChurches.com, Granger's ministry to church leaders, I've come
into contact with several hundred churches of various shapes and sizes.
One thing I've learned along the way is that there appears to be an
inverse relationship between the size of the church and the level of
bureaucracy required to accomplish ministry.

You would expect that the larger a church is, the harder it is to get
anything done. In reality, the opposite seems to be true. Smaller
churches tend to have more boards, more committees, more rules, and
more hoops to jump through. Any new ministry initiative requires
weeks of preliminary discussions and multiple committee votes. For
whatever reason, everyone feels a need to control every aspect of ministry and a call to hold the pastor accountable for everything. So the
pastor doesn't equip the people for ministry; instead, the primary "ministry" role of the people is to control the pastor.

In too many churches, we've confused who is accountable to
whom. Hebrews 13:17 tells us to obey our spiritual leaders and submit
to their authority. In reality, our leaders have a far greater level of
accountability to God than they do to multiple church committees.

The healthy, growing churches I've seen get this right. They give
the pastor great freedom to empower Christ-followers to carry on the

ministry. Ultimately, they recognize that the pastor is called to equip the church to do God's will. Growing churches have far fewer committees and rarely spend time counting votes. Ultimately that means volunteers spend much less time attending meetings and studying *Robert's Rules of Order* than in ministry and studying God's Word.

Please understand that I'm not advocating a dictatorial leadership role for the pastor. I *am* saying that healthy churches don't tie the hands of their pastors, particularly in relation to their day-to-day organizational and spiritual leadership decisions.

> Is your church structure encouraging people to serve in ministry— or in meetings?

If you're hoping to increase the number of volunteers serving in ministry, one of the first things to consider is your church structure. Is it encouraging people to serve in ministry—or in meetings?

Will it help if I put this in the form of a motion? I move that you release people from committee meetings to focus their time, energy, and spiritual gifts on reaching more people for Jesus. May I get a second for that motion?

—Tony

Turf-Guarding Has No Place in the Church

Every one of us has observed a turf battle. You see it in movies when gangs draw imaginary but definite lines and dare anyone to cross over. If you live in or near a large city, every week you read about homicides that are often the result of drug-related turf battles in the inner city.

And it makes me sad to say that most of us have experienced turf battles within the walls of our churches. We build churches with the best of intentions—to show people the love of Christ and to teach them to love others. But then we surround ourselves with a bunch of sin-tarnished human beings (just like ourselves). And, as human beings are apt to do, we begin to erect walls, define our "turf," and bring into the church the style of relating that we've used our whole lives—in society, in our families, and in our workplaces.

> If you drill down to the root of the issue, you'll see that we often view volunteers as property.

Here is how this works. We establish our "territory" (the Sunday school room or certain storage shelves, for example) or our "property" (supplies or materials) or our "people" (volunteers). We draw an imaginary line around "it," and we put up a sign that says, "Keep Off. Do Not Touch. Don't Even Think About It. This Is Mine!" No, it's not a visible sign, but it's made clear to everyone through our attitudes, verbal responses, or body language. People stay away from "it" as they would a minefield. The possibility of causing an explosion just isn't worth it.

I use the word *it* even though we are referring, in part, to volunteers, because that is how we treat them and view them. If you drill down to the root of the issue, you'll see that we often view volunteers as property. "They are on my team. They are my volunteers. Do not talk to them. Do not try to recruit them. I own them." I've actually heard a ministry leader say, "Don't talk to any of my volunteers about your ministry without asking my permission first." I've heard about "keep away" lists of volunteers. "You can recruit anyone in the church to your ministry *except for* those on this list."

Here are some other places where I've seen turf-guarding show up in a church:

Kitchens—We've all seen church kitchens in which every cupboard is labeled with a "do not touch" sign. Cupboard 1: "This belongs to Women's Ministry. Do not touch." Cupboard 2: "This belongs to High School Ministry. Do not touch." Cupboard 3: "This belongs to Seniors' Wednesday Morning Underwater Basket Weaving Class for Widows of Korean Conflict Veterans. Do not touch." And so on. And we all know what happens when we dare to open a restricted cupboard. Sirens sound, alarms go off, and out of nowhere pops Mrs. Snodgrass with a ruler to smack our offending hands. What happened? We crossed into someone else's turf.

Children's Rooms—It can happen in any room in the church, but I've seen it many times in children's classrooms. The teacher comes to you on Sunday morning and says, "Someone was in *my* classroom and went through *my* cupboards, and now I'm missing some of *my* supplies." There is nothing wrong with having volunteers or staff take responsibility for a room to ensure that resources aren't wasted. Turf-guarding shows up, however, in the way we communicate an infraction.

Learn the distinction between turf-guarding and not stealing talent (see Chapter 60, "Don't Steal Talent"). It all comes down to your view of God and your interpretation of the church's purposes.

If you really believe that you are serving one church with one purpose, then you'll realize that everyone is on the same team pulling in the same direction.

If you really believe that we are called to love God *and* others, then the importance of how we treat one another in ministry will become as important as the ministry itself.

If you really believe that all the people in the church should serve in areas about which they are impassioned, excited, and committed, then you will encourage those on your team to continually pursue those things that make their hearts beat fast.

If you really believe that God is sovereign, that he is still on the throne, and that he is the one who is all-knowing (not you), then you will trust him when people move on or off your team.

I once asked Byron, my former boss at Life Action Ministries, how he was able to maintain his calm at a time when so many good people were leaving his team. He taught me a valuable lesson: "I really believe that God is in charge, and if a high-capacity person is leaving, then God has someone even better in store for us."

Let's hang on to God tightly and to one another loosely. And let's stop the turf-guarding in our churches.

—Tim

Have Your Kids Help Load the Winnebago

"But as for me and my family, we will serve the Lord"
(JOSHUA 24:15b, NLT).

I have pictures to prove it. When I was in high school, I was in a Christian rock band. Our group was called Burning Heart—not so much for the warming of the Holy Spirit inside the heart as for the sense of heartburn or indigestion that people experienced when listening to our music. In other words, we weren't very good.

Though our musical talent left something to be desired, we did get several gigs one summer that prompted the Burning Heart tour. The parents of our guitar player owned a Winnebago that we would load up with all of our equipment and head off to play for area youth groups. We even had "roadies" to help us load and unload the camper. My little brother was one of them. He didn't know Jesus at the time, but he was more than able to move instruments, and he loved the classic Burning Heart hits that made us the rage in church basements throughout Southwest Ohio.

Somewhere between our first concert at Washington Elementary School and our final tour stop, my brother learned what it was to have a relationship with Jesus. He had been watching our band pray and worship together, and the message finally clicked for him. Through serving in a unique way with my brother, I got to witness his life transformed for eternity.

Do you have opportunities for families of all ages to serve in ministry? At Granger, we have dads serving with their sons in our traffic ministry. We have moms serving with their teenage daughters in children's ministry. We have opportunities for families to serve together in local missions. By providing these opportunities, we are able to help parents model some important values for their children:

- Parents demonstrate the importance of following through with commitments. The kids learn that sometimes you have to help others even when you don't feel like it.
- Parents model finding a ministry and serving Jesus. The children learn that being connected in a church is more about giving their time to reach others than about receiving the benefits of membership.
- Children learn the basics of teamwork. They learn how to fulfill their specific roles to accomplish a greater good.
- When families serve together, they build memories together. Their experiences in ministry will remind both kids and parents how fun it can be to serve Jesus by serving others.

Children won't fit into every ministry role, but there are many ways that parents and their children can serve together. Whether it's directing traffic, serving meals to the homeless, or packing a Winnebago for the next concert tour, invite your kids or younger siblings along for the experience.

—Tony

12

Let People Observe

What goes through people's minds when they're thinking about stepping into ministry at your church?

"How do I know what I'll like?"

"Once I sign up, I'll never be able to get out of it."

"What if I do it for three weeks and discover I hate it? How will I ever get out of it once they are counting on me?"

"What if I like the ministry, but the people I'm working with are weird? I'd never be able to say that, and I'd be stuck."

Most of these thoughts will never be expressed out loud, but they are definitely being thought. Part of effective communication is to figure out what questions will come to mind when people are being asked to volunteer—and then to answer them in your presentation. Here is what we do at Granger.

We say what people are thinking. We acknowledge their fears. We'll say something like this: "Some of you right now are scared to death. You've been burned. You've volunteered for something before, and then you were stuck there for years. Some of you are thinking, 'What if I don't like the role?' or 'What if I don't like the people you stick me with?' We want you to know that we think these are valid concerns, so here's what we've done. The first week that you serve, you will do so as an observer. You can roam to different areas and check out different roles. You can see what fits you…"

This quickly puts people at ease. They don't feel threatened by bait-and-switch tactics. It calms their fears.

Nearly every week, someone with an "observer" nametag will be in our children's classrooms. Observers are there to see *what* they like and to see *who* they like. Sometimes they remain in the observer role for a few weeks in a row. Most of the time, they end up slipping into a permanent role. Occasionally, they determine that it isn't a fit, and they look for another place to serve.

This is a win-win strategy. You want your volunteers to be happy! If they're in roles in which they excel and they're with people they like, they are likely to serve happily for a long time. When that happens, the leader can rely on the volunteer, and the ministry is fruitful!

—Tim

E-Volunteers Make Good Servers

One of the most amazing things I've witnessed in the church over the last several years is how technology is reshaping the direction of ministry. There are now countless ways that people can serve without having to set foot on your campus. With a high-speed Internet connection and a home computer, your virtual volunteer team is just a few mouse clicks away.

Here are some examples of ministry roles that are taking place outside the walls of our church using today's technology:

Web Maintenance—We have volunteers who are creating graphics, drafting content, and adding programming updates to our Web sites. Functionality has been developed so that volunteers don't have to know computer programming in order to keep the sites up to date with current ministry information.

Editing/Proofing—We have volunteers who are solely responsible for editing and proofing communications such as the weekend bulletin, fliers, and newsletter articles. A writer e-mails the documents, and the proofing team makes sure we done good with our grammar skills. (Just making sure *our* editor is still paying attention!)

E-Mail Inquiries—We also have a team of volunteers responsible for handling the e-mail inquiries we receive. That includes e-mail from people who attend our church and from others who are just curious to learn more about our ministry. This team has Web access to the e-mail accounts and can respond to inquiries from any computer with an Internet connection.

Prayer Web—At Granger, well over one hundred prayer ministry volunteers receive weekly prayer requests by e-mail. Remember the days when your prayer ministry team had a list of people to telephone for emergency prayer requests? Now those prayer needs can be instantly distributed to the entire team by e-mail.

Facility Scheduling—Web solutions are now available that will allow your volunteers to request and manage facility space from remote locations. Check out ServiceU (www.serviceu.com) to see an example. Volunteers can manage rooms and resources, publish events to your Web site, and process registrations without ever going to your church offices.

The list could go on and on. The point is that, through technology, volunteers are no longer limited to certain hours to participate in your ministry efforts. E-volunteers reduce the need for office space and office equipment, and they multiply the amount of ministry that can be accomplished. You may not know how to find the technology to make it happen, but I can guarantee you that people in your church do, or they know someone who can help out.

> Through technology, volunteers are no longer limited to certain hours to participate in your ministry efforts.

Don't *cybernate* (hibernate from the Web) while technology passes you by. Take advantage of the Web and e-volunteers to link your ministry to your servers.

—Tony

Teach Shoulder-Tapping

14

Melissa had been the lead teacher in the preschool room since September. Now Thanksgiving was approaching, and she was still short-handed. Every time she met with her volunteers, they would say the same thing: "You need to tell the pastor that he has to get us more help in here!" And every time she met with Pastor Johnson, she would deliver the message: "My volunteers are dying! We need more help. Please stand up this Sunday and ask for more volunteers. Tell them the children deserve our best." Pastor Johnson would sympathize with Melissa and assure her again that he was working on it and would continue to ask the congregation.

What's wrong with this picture? First, Melissa believes that it is Pastor Johnson's role to recruit new volunteers for her ministry. Second, Melissa's volunteers also believe that. And third, Pastor Johnson has communicated by his actions that he believes it as well! The entire culture of that church supports the idea that Pastor Johnson is responsible for recruiting new volunteers.

If the pastors or church staff members are the ones solely responsible for finding and placing new volunteers, then the growth of the church will be limited. Why? Because very few people will respond to pleas for help. (Tony talked about this in Chapter 1, "Don't Ask For Help.") Rather, most will jump in and help either because *they want to make a difference with their lives* or because *they want deeper relational connections with others*.

That's why you must teach "shoulder-tapping." All leaders and volunteers must believe that it is their responsibility to "tap the shoulders" of the folks next to them and invite them into ministry. I'm not referring to the people sitting next to them on Sunday morning, but the people standing next to them in life—the people with whom they are in relationship. It is so inviting to hear, "Join me." This tells me that someone wants to be with me, that I have worth, that I can make a difference.

Every volunteer in my ministry area has contacts that I don't have. They have nurtured friendships and developed relationships that are different from mine. For that reason, the shoulders they tap will be within a unique network of relationships.

Just try this. If you tell each volunteer in your church that in the next year it is his or her job to "tap the shoulder" of one person who is not currently serving, you will double your team within one year! Wouldn't that be fantastic? Now, in reality, many of your seasoned volunteers (those who have been in the church for a number of years) won't find anyone because all of their friends are already serving. They've "tapped out" all of their relationships and haven't been nurturing new relationships with the unchurched. However, some of those who are new in your church will make up for it by tapping ten, twelve, or more friends.

If you're really brave, let your volunteers tap the shoulders of those who don't attend your church. What a great way to build a relationship with seekers in your community! (For more on this idea, read Chapter 44, "Easy Access Is Crucial.")

The next time Melissa meets with her team, she can ask, "Who do you know who you could invite to serve with you next week?" This simple question will turn her team into a proactive, problem-solving group rather than a blame-casting, complaining one. Sounds like a good change to me.

—Tim

15

Real Leaders Lead Volunteers

"He who thinks he leads, but has no followers, is only taking a walk."
—*JOHN C. MAXWELL* [1]

Having spent several years in leadership roles in the marketplace prior to moving into ministry, I know firsthand that there are unique challenges to both environments. In the marketplace, for example, leaders face the challenges of leading people who don't share a Christ-centered perspective. That influences decision making as well as relational interactions. Though we Christ-followers are still human and make stupid mistakes from time to time, my experience has been that the working environment in ministry is much more positive. Also, people in ministry generally make better and more consistent decisions because those decisions are based on a set of core values driven by their walk with Christ.

In the marketplace, a good leader tries to earn the respect of those he or she leads, but those working for the leader follow directions because they are paid to do so. The bottom line for many employees in paid roles is that they work to take home a paycheck. Though money can't be the only motivating factor in the marketplace, it does give a leader the leverage that leaders of volunteers don't have. Additionally, if people don't work out or if they just aren't a good fit for a particular position, it's a lot easier to fire someone you've hired than someone who has volunteered.

That's why I think the true test of leadership is leading volunteers. Volunteers don't serve in order to get a paycheck. Neither do they follow because someone has a leadership title. That's why leaders of volunteers must be able to communicate a compelling vision and effectively focus ministry efforts toward fulfilling that vision. These leaders must help people find their core purpose and match them to ministry roles in which they feel valued. They must help volunteers find and pursue their unique calling.

Leading volunteers requires a different type of leader. Rather than focusing on positional leadership, a good ministry leader will excel in developing collaboration, giving volunteers appropriate ownership, and creating authentic relationships where team-based ministry is the expectation and not just something that's talked about. Leaders of volunteers do much more coaching than dictating. It's that leadership style that keeps volunteers in the game.

It's still possible for a command-and-control leader to survive in the marketplace. There are certainly more effective leadership styles for most work environments, but that type of leader can still make it. That same leader, however, won't last long leading volunteers in ministry. Because volunteers have the easy option to walk away from a serving opportunity, it's in a leader's best interest to focus on an approach that brings out the best in those giving their time and gifts. Otherwise, the ministry leader is likely to find he or she is the one just taking a walk.

—Tony

ENDNOTE

1. John C. Maxwell, *The 21 Irrefutable Laws of Leadership* (Nashville, TN: Thomas Nelson, Inc., 1998), 20.

The Attraction Factor

first met my wife in 1988. I occasionally reflect on what initially attracted me to her. During those early days when it truly was "love at first sight," what were the characteristics I saw that caused me to want to spend the rest of my life with her? Don't get me wrong—I can think of plenty. It's just hard to narrow it down from all the things that I now love about her. I remember telling a friend, "I've never met someone whose beauty emanates from so deeply within her." Maybe that was it.

Have you ever thought about what attracts people to your church? Or to your ministry team? Why do they join? Why do they stay?

I believe three main factors attract or repel potential team members:

The Vision—It is the vision that draws people. Proverbs 29:18 says "Where there is no vision, the people perish" (King James Version). People want their lives to matter. They want to make a difference, so they "sign on" to a vision to do something or go somewhere or accomplish something.

The Leader—You may love the vision, but if you don't respect the leader, you probably won't sign on to the team. We all need to know if the leader can lead and if he or she possesses integrity and honesty. We've all been in positions in which someone says (either verbally or through their actions), "I like the vision...I just don't like you."

The Team—People have to know that the people they are working with are like them. If they love the vision and respect the leader but think the team is a bunch of knuckleheads, then they probably won't stick around.

However, the order in which people evaluate these elements is not always the same:

Leader-Vision-Team—People attracted to a new church or other organization are usually attracted at first by the leader, then by the vision, and finally by the team. This is because they typically meet the leader before they ever hear the vision. They won't take time to hear the vision or meet the team if they don't like the leader.

Vision-Leader-Team—In a more established organization, it is often the vision that first attracts, then the leader, and then the team. That is because the vision is being communicated at many levels by a variety of people or methods, and it is the vision that is driving the organization. At Granger, people can sign on to the vision, and then it might be months or years before they personally spend time with the senior pastor. But they love the vision, and they've found a leader elsewhere in the church to whom they are connected.

Team-Vision-Leader—Sometimes a high-performing team's reputation precedes it. The team is known by its unity, focus, capacity, performance, and results. People want to be challenged by, and identified with, that kind of team.

Whatever the order, be aware of the "attraction factor" in your organization. If you know what draws individuals to your team, you'll be better able to keep them.

—Tim

Choose Proven Leaders

"Unless you are faithful in small matters,
you won't be faithful in large ones. If you cheat even a little,
you won't be honest with greater responsibilities"
(LUKE 16:10, NLT).

Do you want to kill a ministry program really fast? The easiest way to do it is to make a mistake when selecting leadership for that ministry. In Chapter 43, we describe the danger of considering availability over ability. That error is magnified when you are trying to identify people for leadership roles.

I've run into people who are genuinely passionate about a particular ministry area and want to help expand it to reach more people. The problem is that they want the pastor to design the ministry strategy, cast vision to the church, recruit help, and participate in ongoing programming. Don't launch new ministries until you've identified someone else to fill those roles. A good volunteer leader will take responsibilities off the pastor's plate rather than adding to it.

Here are some suggestions for identifying volunteers with leadership ability:

> A good volunteer leader will take responsibilities off the pastor's plate rather than adding to it.

Find people who have led smaller groups. If people have successfully led a home group, Bible study, or task team, they are more likely to succeed in leading larger groups that include other leaders. Find people who have shown they can lead and influence others in smaller settings before you put them in charge of larger ministries. As Paul suggested to Timothy, people "should be given other responsibilities in the church as a test of their character and ability" (from 1 Timothy 3:10, NLT). If people prove they can handle small roles, then you can give them more responsibility.

Always ask, "Is anyone following them now?" Leaders naturally attract other people. Though people may not occupy formal leadership roles, you'll know they have leadership potential by the number of people who are already following them. Do people gather around them before and after services? Do they influence the decisions of others for social activities? Do they tend to include others in their daily activities?

Then ask, "Who is following them now?" Are the people following them the ones you're hoping to attract to a particular ministry area? If not, then the potential leaders will not likely change whom they attract when they're in leadership roles. Typically you attract people who are like you. That's why it's so important to consider who appears on the platform during your weekend services from week to week. The same holds true in sub-ministries throughout the church. People gathered in large groups will probably reflect their leadership teams, and that's why you should consider the diversity of your team to make sure it reflects the community you are trying to reach.

Look for people who have demonstrated leadership ability in the marketplace. Obviously there are biblical guidelines to consider when selecting leaders in the church (see 1 Timothy 3:1-12 and Titus 1:6-9 for examples), but I think we often overlook the obvious. If God has granted a person leadership gifts, then he or she will probably be demonstrating leadership skills in the marketplace. Even if these people aren't spiritually prepared for a leadership role, identify them and create a discipleship process to prepare them to leverage their leadership gifts in ministry.

People need to demonstrate the capacity for leadership before they receive increasing leadership responsibilities. This principle may not hold true for selecting the governor of California or Minnesota, but it should hold true in your ministry.

—Tony

Dispel the Myth of the Superpastor

"It was he who gave some...to be pastors and teachers,
to prepare God's people for works of service,
so that the body of Christ may be built up"
(EPHESIANS 4:11-12).

It's a common myth in churches: We hire pastors to *do* ministry. If they can't get it done, then they hire staff to help them. Of course, there are always a few fanatics in the church who will also help, but for the most part we rely on the pastors to do the ministry.

It's called the Superpastor Myth. We convince ourselves that the pastor has a special connection to God and has been endowed with "pastor dust." Being in his or her very presence is enough to make a person more spiritual. If the pastor isn't the one doing the talking or visiting or caring or leading...then it's just not good enough.

It's *typical* for seminaries to perpetuate the myth. In fact, many of them have spent decades training "doers" rather than "leaders."

It's *convenient* for the laity to believe the myth. It makes it so much easier to remain uninvolved and critical of someone else for not getting the work done.

It's *heady* for the pastor to believe it. Who doesn't want to be a superhero?

We do unintentional things to perpetuate the myth. We ask Superpastor to pray before every church meal. If he's in the room, then it's up to him to bless the beans. We expect Superpastor to visit us in the hospital. No one else will be able to say the right things at the right time. Superpastor offers financial counseling, career counseling, parenting and marriage counseling, crisis counseling, and every other kind of counseling. Only a superpastor could be an expert in all those areas.

What if pastors really took the Ephesians passage seriously? What if we saw it as our responsibility from God to equip the believers for ministry? What if we trained our members to run meetings, teach lessons, lead small groups, visit people in the hospital, offer care, and provide counseling? What if we measured our success by how often we were *equipping* and measured our failure by how often we were *doing*?

> What if we measured our success by how often we were *equipping* and measured our failure by how often we were *doing*?

What if it were our goal to push the ministry as far out into the church as possible? What if we agreed upon the mission, vision, and values that we share, and then we just let people go? What would happen if an individual in crisis were offered help by a trained leader who was already in relationship with him or her?

And then, as the church grows, what if our purpose as pastors transitioned toward training trainers and leading leaders? What if, rather than *adding* leaders, we could be *multiplying* leaders?

Let's kill the myth of the superpastor. Let's show our church that we are human beings placed in a position to lead the church. Let's adopt the value that every member is a minister and that significance and fulfillment in the Christian life come through serving.

—Tim

19

If You Don't Need a Volunteer, You're in Trouble

"The harvest is plentiful, but the workers are few. Ask the Lord of the harvest, therefore, to send out workers into his harvest field"

(LUKE 10:2).

Can you imagine the U.S. Army turning away prospective recruits? Can you imagine walking into a post office and seeing posters of Uncle Sam saying, "We don't need you"? Imagine another army around Christmastime. What if the Salvation Army started turning people away? "No, we don't need your help. We have enough people to ring the bells this year." What if Jimmy Carter started turning people away from Habitat for Humanity projects? What if he said, "No, we have enough volunteers to construct this house. Please find another way to use your time and resources"?

We can't imagine these scenarios. All of these organizations constantly communicate the vision that anyone can help, anytime. The church needs to operate with the same vision. We can't afford to ever tell someone we aren't accepting new volunteers. A particular person may not be gifted to serve in a certain role, but there will always be some way for him or her to serve. There should always be opportunities in every ministry area for qualified volunteers to step in and serve. If you close the door on all volunteers, people will begin to assume they're not needed. In the long run, that will jeopardize your ability to recruit when you really need the support.

With that in mind, here are some questions to consider when you think you have enough volunteers:

Am I doing too much? You may have too much on your plate.

Consider the tasks you could give away to volunteers, and keep the three or four roles that allow you to add the most value to the ministry. As a ministry leader, you should be focusing most of your time on leadership. By releasing some of your responsibilities to others, you will have more time to concentrate on what you do best.

Could this become a team effort? One person may be filling a role that would be better filled by a team. In our creative-arts ministry, for example, there are roles for people who can't sing or play an instrument but have a passion for the arts. They help out in the office with administrative tasks. They serve on our stage crew. They serve other church leaders who come to learn about our arts ministry at workshops and conferences. In other words, there are ways to divide up ministry roles so more people can serve and feel connected to a team (see Chapter 3, "Just Chunk It").

Do I have enough leaders? Sometimes you can't imagine adding another volunteer to your team because you already have too many for whom you provide care. You're already dropping too many balls because there are too many people seeking direction from you. If this is the case, you should be focusing on finding volunteers who can take on leadership responsibilities. These are the volunteers who multiply your time. While leading and caring for other volunteers, they remove tasks from your plate.

> The church can't afford to have "Not Hiring" signs posted on the front door.

Is my vision too small? Maybe you haven't stepped back in a while to consider what God could do if more gifted people were on the team. How could your ministry increase its impact? How could you reach more people in the community? How could you more effectively help people take faith steps? This doesn't necessarily require the creation of more ministry programming. It may simply involve looking for opportunities to improve what you're already doing to reach people for Jesus.

When people serve in ministry, they're more likely to focus on their walk with Christ. They're more likely to invite others. They're more likely to give financially. They're more likely to stay connected to the mission and vision. The church can't afford to have "Not Hiring" signs posted on the front door. You need to continuously create ways to connect more and more people into meaningful ministry.

—Tony

Build a Replacement Mind-Set

Around Granger, we often joke about the last line in every staff member's job description: *"Perform other duties as requested."* That pretty much covers everything.

"Go wash my car. It's in your job description."

"It is?"

"Yep, last line."

"When you've finished, run around the building three times, and then come inside and pour my coffee."

"OK, it's in my job description."

Fortunately our supervisors aren't autocratic, and the staff isn't stupid. But we do have fun with that line.

What would it be like if the last line in the ministry description of every volunteer was something like this: "Work yourself out of a position"? What if volunteers started in their ministry roles knowing that one of their primary responsibilities was to find someone to take their place? How would the culture of your church be affected if all the volunteers knew they could—and should—recruit, mentor, and train others to take their place?

Of course you must have systems in place to ensure that these folks are qualified to replace their mentors. You must take your singers and musicians through an audition process. You want to make sure that the background of every adult who works with kids or students has been checked. Wouldn't it be fun, though, if your volunteers were constantly introducing you to people who have been groomed to take their place?

Imagine hearing these words frequently rather than rarely: "This is Bob. I've trained him to take my place. He sat beside me for several weeks, watching and taking notes. For the past few weeks, he's been filling the role by himself, and I've been sitting beside him to offer support and encouragement. He is now fully trained, and I'm ready for a new assignment!" What a fun conversation that would be!

This is not just a cool idea that will get you a steady flow of new volunteers. It is also a great motivator for certain types of leaders. Many people are wired for challenges; they don't like maintenance. Once they've learned something and succeeded at it, they're ready to move on. By adding the "replace yourself" line to their ministry descriptions, they'll have four challenges instead of just one. *First*, they must learn and master the roles they've been assigned. *Second*, they must find people who could fill their roles. *Third*, they must train their replacements. And *finally*, they must be prepared for the challenges of a new role.

However, just as some people require this kind of built-in challenge, others will read the "replace yourself" line and drop dead in front of you. They would consider drinking battery acid before they would ask anything of anybody. So be a student of people. Don't be afraid to set the bar high and give people a challenge, but if you notice that they haven't exhaled in ten or twelve minutes, then you may want to ease up and find a different approach.

I have to stop writing now. I have to buy a gift for my boss's brother's mother-in-law's birthday. It's in my job description, you know.

—Tim

21

Learn How People Are Wired

> "God has given gifts to each of you from his great variety of spiritual gifts. Manage them well so that God's generosity can flow through you"
> *(1 PETER 4:10, NLT).*

When I was growing up, I loved baseball. I spent many summer days in the backyard playing with the neighborhood kids. We played so often that large dirt spots began to form around the bases and the pitcher's mound. Dad could never get the grass to grow in those areas.

I used to lie in bed at night listening to the Cincinnati Reds games. Those were the days of the "Big Red Machine." My heroes were guys like Pete Rose, Johnny Bench, and Joe Morgan. I used to dream of the day I might walk out onto the field of Riverfront Stadium for a big game against the Los Angeles Dodgers. I wouldn't fall asleep until I knew the final score and heard Joe Nuxhall, the radio announcer, sign off by saying, "This is the ol' left-hander rounding third and heading for home."

The only problem with my love of baseball was the fact that I really didn't have much talent. I wasn't a very good fielder. I tried pitching but failed miserably. I was pretty slow, so I wasn't much on the base paths. Once I started playing with older kids, I found that I was afraid of the ball, so I ended up being a poor hitter. So what do you do when you love baseball but you can't field, you can't pitch, you can't run, and you can't hit? You take up golf.

> The only problem with my love of baseball was the fact that I really didn't have much talent.

Fortunately, Christ-followers are promised spiritual gifts. Our responsibility as leaders is to help those around us identify their gifts and use them. "God has given each of us the ability to do certain things well" (Romans 12:6, NLT). Paul goes on in that passage to exhort us to use these gifts well and to take our roles seriously.

As you work at equipping others, identify a process to help people learn how they are wired. This process should include a method for helping them discover their spiritual gifts. One way people learn how they've been gifted is by jumping into different ministry roles. This helps them find out what they do well and what they'd prefer to leave for someone else.

You can also help people narrow their focus by offering tools designed to identify their gifts. One resource is the NetWork curriculum developed at Willow Creek Community Church (www.willowcreek.com). Or you might check out Rick Warren's "Class 301" materials (www.pastors.com) that he developed to help people identify their SHAPEs—spiritual gifts, heart, abilities, personality, and experiences. Warren has challenged us to consider that there's far more to identifying people's ministry fit than just discovering their spiritual gifts. Similarly, Fellowship Church in Grapevine, Texas, has partnered with the Giftedness Center in Dallas (www.thegiftednesscenter.com) to create the "Discover Your Design" ministry to help people discover their unique designs for ministry.

By helping people learn how they are wired, you'll improve the likelihood that your volunteers will experience fulfillment in their ministry roles. Your ministry effectiveness will increase, and, more important, you'll find that the number of golfers in your church will decline. For us ex-baseball players trying to get a tee time, that's a good thing.

—Tony

22

Take the Blame and Give the Credit

I am the youngest member of my family. My brother, Joe, is more than four years older than I am. That definitely gave him the advantage when he was seventeen and I was only thirteen. However, in recent years I've enjoyed pointing out to him that he is in his forties, and I'm still a young thirty-something.

My sister, Dena, is thirteen months older than I am. Due to school cut-off dates, she had the distinct privilege of going through school with her little brother in the same grade and class all the way through our senior year. Pretty lucky, huh?

Those of us who are the "babies" of the family share a little lie. We claim that anytime something happened in the family, it was the oldest child who thought of it, the middle child who did it, and the youngest child who was blamed. That's right—I was the victim of the cruelty of my big brother and big sister.

The truth is, however, that I initiated and executed much of the wrongdoing without any help. It didn't require someone else to think it up for me. There was plenty of blame that rightfully belonged to me as I dreamed up new ways to test my boundaries and stretch the rules.

Taking the blame may be a misnomer about the youngest kids in the house, but it is the privilege of leadership. You get to say, "I'm sorry it happened that way" or "I apologize that you were offended by us" even when you were not personally involved in the offense.

The fastest way to reduce the size of your team is to abandon it when a mistake is made. If you allow a volunteer to look bad while you remain removed or uninvolved, it can mean only one thing: You are insecure. You lack confidence and maturity, and your leadership days are numbered. People will not follow for long if they think their leader is looking out only for his or her own interests.

When a volunteer says something that is inappropriate or unkind, address it with the individual privately, but take the blame publicly. When a volunteer messes up and overspends the budget by $500, work with the person privately to make sure it won't happen again, but take the blame publicly. When your technical volunteers miss an audio cue or turn the lights on at the wrong time, do more training privately, but take the blame publicly.

Of course, there are limits to this principle. If people continue to mess up, they may need to be removed from your team. Even so, you can still shield their character while finding other places for them to serve. When the issue is sin rather than human error, however, you must deal with it quickly and let the blame fall on the individuals. As part of their healing and restoration, they will need to feel the consequences of their actions.

Just as you should take the blame for mistakes, you should also give away credit for successes. Take every opportunity to spotlight people on your team who are contributing to the ministry. Anytime you are given credit publicly or thanked for your leadership, always use that opportunity to deflect the glory to God and the thanks to your team.

> The only way to become more secure in your leadership is to develop the disciplines and habits of a secure leader.

If this is hard for you and you struggle with insecurity, then just push through it. The only way to become more secure in your leadership is to develop the disciplines and habits of a secure leader.

So start practicing. Take the blame and give the credit. It might never feel *natural*, but it will feel *right* and will increase others' respect of your leadership.

—Tim

Have a Fair

One of the most effective ways we've found to place people in volunteer roles is to periodically hold ministry fairs. We do this once or twice a year during all five of our weekend services. We ask representatives from all the ministries in the church to set up tables with information about their teams and the specific roles available to those who would like to serve. Through the creative use of decorations, media, and handouts, the teams share their stories and answer questions.

The best thing about the fairs is that they give a general overview of all the serving opportunities available in the church. In just a few minutes, people can stop at a handful of tables and learn what ministries might best fit their gifts and passions. Additionally, the fairs attract people who could be helped by the ministries. For example, one person may discover how to lead a small group, while another person may learn something that encourages him or her to *join* a small group. It's a win-win situation for those who want to serve and for those who are served.

If you decide to hold a ministry fair, consider the following suggestions:

- Couple the fair with a message that helps people understand why they might want to serve. (See an example in Chapter 42, "Use Your 'Bully Pulpit.' ")
- Place signs directing people to the ministry areas represented at the fair.
- Be sure to distribute handouts summarizing the roles in which people may serve.

- Create a way for people to sign up. Then have your team follow up immediately. This point is critical. Make sure the systems are in place for follow-up *before* you start asking people to sign up. (See Chapter 40, "Don't Drop the Ball.")
- Plan the next step. Will people be able to serve immediately? Will you hold an informational meeting to give interested people more details? Will you hold a training session? Will you create "observer" roles to give people opportunities to see what they like? (See Chapter 12, "Let People Observe.")
- Remind team leaders that they're not competing with other ministries for volunteers. Instead, they should be focused on helping people find ministry connections that match their skills, experiences, and personalities.

Ministry fairs focus on those who are unconnected and are looking for ways to serve, rather than on specific ministries' volunteer needs. In this setting, people can narrow their inquiries to those teams that match their gifts and interests. And with so many choices available, the number of ministry connections will increase.

Though the retention rate of connections made through ministry fairs is not as high as those made through shoulder-tapping (see Chapter 14, "Teach Shoulder-Tapping"), these fairs are a great way to promote an atmosphere of volunteerism within the church. So what about it? Is it time for your church to have a fair?

—Tony

You'll Never Have Enough Staff

It's that time of year again: budget time. It's a time to reflect on what God has accomplished during the past year, dream about possibilities for the coming year, and gear up for another year of ministry.

Budget time is also a difficult time because every year, regardless of how much the offerings have increased, we never have enough money to accomplish *all* of our goals. We can never hire enough staff to do everything as efficiently and effectively as we believe is necessary.

Whether yours is a church of a hundred, a thousand, or ten thousand, if your goal is to accomplish the Great Commission, you will never have enough staff. Here are some tips for dealing with this reality:

Hire only when you absolutely must. I've been to churches in which the pastors do everything and the church members see it as their responsibility to warm the pews and "keep the pastor accountable." Where is that in the Bible? Instead of agonizing over how to find the money to hire staff, spend your time figuring out how to motivate the members to take part in ministry. Follow some of the other tips in this book such as "Have a Fair" (Chapter 23), "Teach Shoulder-Tapping" (Chapter 14), and "Use Your 'Bully Pulpit' " (Chapter 42).

Create a culture in which volunteers do it before staff. Your church may have a long and rich tradition of laziness. The pastors or leaders who preceded you may have bought into the lie that they were supposed to do everything. They may have spent their time teaching the congregation about the nuances of transubstantiation, but forgot to mention that God wants them actively involved in the lives of others. It may take months or years to transform your church into an army of volunteers that influences your community through service and love.

Don't shy away from letting volunteers give significant amounts of time. There are people in your church who have the discretionary time to give ten, fifteen, twenty, or more hours a week as volunteers. They may be single, retired, empty nesters, or unemployed. At Granger, scores of people give huge amounts of time to the church. Virgil is recently retired and spends hours in the office each week helping with administrative tasks. Augie is sometimes at the church fifteen or more hours a week practicing and playing with the band. Greg gives scores of hours each month helping our lighting and maintenance teams.

Take care of your staff, but make heroes of the volunteers. If you read our first book, *Simply Strategic Stuff,* you know we are passionate about taking care of the staff. It's crucial to care for those who have given their lives to serve the church. Make sure, though, that you don't unintentionally communicate that the staff members are the heroes or that a volunteer hasn't "arrived" until he or she is on staff. Make sure you are constantly communicating this truth: "The heroes in this church are the volunteers!"

If you think you're the exception and you have enough staff, then you need to get a bigger dream. Are all the people within driving distance of your church already following Christ, growing in their faith, and taking steps in their spiritual journey? Do they all have the five purposes of the church at work in their lives? No? I didn't think so. If you think you have enough staff, you may need to ask God for the perspective to see the need around you!

It's healthy to not get everything we want. This forces us to rely on God. It drives us into prayer. It motivates us to build teams. It causes us to look for the giftedness in others. It nurtures our creativity. It helps us prioritize. It keeps our feet grounded in reality.

So the next time you're frustrated by your church's limitations, think about the last spoiled-rotten teenager you were around who got everything he or she wanted. Reality makes you bearable.

—Tim

It's Not All About You

"So now I am giving you a new commandment: Love each other. Just as I have loved you, you should love each other. Your love for one another will prove to the world that you are my disciples" *(JOHN 13:34-35, NLT).*

Have you ever noticed that people look at church in two very different ways? (Their outlooks probably reflect how they look at life in general.) They either look at a ministry and ask, "What do you have for me?" or they look at others and ask, "How can I serve you?"

Don't get me wrong. We should all be concerned with our own spiritual development, relational connections, and the ministries that influence our children, for example. It's not appropriate, however, when those desires supersede God's command to love others. The "feed me" view of the church isn't biblical. Instead, we should be focused on feeding others—both as a church and as individuals within the church.

This is one of those principles that you'll need to remind people about from time to time. You'll need to come right out and say, "Remember, it's not about us. It's about the people we're trying to reach for Jesus. It's about the people we're trying to help take their next steps toward Christ. It's about helping the hurting and the hopeless. It's about being Jesus to the community around us."

If you regularly revisit this part of your church's vision, you'll notice several positive changes in your congregation:

You'll turn off people who are focused on themselves. This is good because they'll either recognize the sin in their lives and change their focus, or they'll leave your church. In either instance, you and the people Jesus is calling your church to reach will win.

The focus on others will be attractive to people who are seeking purpose for their lives. People want to invest their time and resources in ways that will positively influence the lives of others.

You'll create a friendly environment for new guests. When the focus is on others, those currently connected in your ministry will constantly be viewing everything that happens around the church from the perspective of a newcomer. That will improve your church's atmosphere and generate a more welcoming environment.

> When the focus is on others, those currently connected in your ministry will constantly be viewing everything that happens around the church from the perspective of a newcomer.

At Granger we frequently find that the people who are most prone to lose proper focus have come from other churches with expectations that Granger will operate as their previous churches did. But Granger has an untraditional approach to ministry, so these folks are sometimes disappointed and may try to "fix" us. We treat these instances as learning opportunities, and we try to remind people about the mission and vision to which God has called us. Some embrace the vision, and others do not. We don't, however, make changes to try to make people happy when those changes would move us off course from God's plan for Granger Community Church.

This is primarily a communications function. You'll need to remind the church often about the importance of focusing on others. Jesus told us that this one principle would clearly set apart the disciples of Christ. While the culture shouts, "It's all about me," the church must stand firm in its commitment to focus on others.

—Tony

The More
the Merrier

On January 4, 2003, our church received four truckloads of food from Feed the Children (www.feedthechildren.org). Each week during December, the people of our church had brought extra offerings for this project, and by the end of December we had more than enough money to provide this gift of over one hundred thousand pounds of food to the city of South Bend. There was excitement in the air all month long!

The food bank that was taking the delivery was able to supply forklifts and personnel to unload the truck. They asked us to have five or ten volunteers available to assist them. That was it. No one else was needed. Pretty efficient, huh?

But wait! We wanted to provide a "moment" for our people. We wanted to create an event they would remember for the rest of their lives. We wanted to see parents and their kids unloading food for hungry children. We wanted people to do more than give money. We wanted the people of the church to see the results, to work with their hands, and to look into the eyes of those who were receiving the food. It wasn't about efficiency; it was about making memories and watching lives change as our people invested their time in a worthy cause.

And it was a party. Although it was barely ten degrees on that January morning, more than four hundred people showed up to unload the trucks. We purposely parked the trucks quite a distance from the building because we wanted everyone to participate. We formed a line that allowed everyone to touch the boxes as they were passed hand to hand from the backs of the trucks into the building. There were tears and laughter. All three local television stations showed up to report. One of the morning shows was so blown away by this outrageous act of kindness that it broadcast over fifteen minutes of live reports and interviews. We had enough volunteers to personally deliver a box of food and personal items to *every single* government-subsidized housing project in a two-county area.

What is the principle? Look for opportunities to involve your people in hands-on ministry. Scores of those who showed up had never been involved as volunteers before, yet we created an opportunity for them to make a difference with their time while building relationships with others in the church.

> Look for opportunities to involve your people in hands-on ministry.

Would it have been easier to coordinate ten people and a forklift? Absolutely. As it was, we had to figure out parking, the exact arrival time of the trucks, coordination with the press, organization of the unloading, maps for food deliveries, and a hundred other small details. But it was worth it.

And the celebration didn't stop that day. All year long, people talked about the excitement of that frigid January day. One year later, even more people wanted to help. Over one thousand showed up on the first Saturday of 2004 to unload nine truckloads of food (over two hundred tons!) for area charities. Once again we left the forklifts inside and gave everyone a chance to participate!

Sometimes the best way to accomplish something is with just a few people so that everyone can stay focused on ministry. Many times, however, the more the merrier. Don't miss a chance to create an unforgettable moment.

—Tim

Limit Your Span of Care

"Then he selected twelve of them to be his regular companions, calling them apostles. He sent them out to preach"
(MARK 3:14, NLT).

I love the fact that we can learn so many key leadership strategies directly from Jesus himself. Prior to the events described in this verse in Mark 3, Jesus had been teaching before a large gathering. In fact, so many had gathered to hear him that he had a boat ready in case he was crowded off the beach. But Jesus' ministry went beyond just proclaiming truth to the masses. He also had a strategic plan in mind to build a church that would bring the gospel to the world. Instead of gathering as many people as possible to make that happen, Jesus narrowed his relational focus to

> If Jesus chose twelve, how many do you think should be in your circle of regular companions?

only a handful of committed followers and servants—the twelve apostles. Knowing they would carry on the ministry after his death, he poured his time into these people to reach the world. Jesus had twelve on his immediate team.

If Jesus chose twelve, how many do you think should be in your circle of regular companions? How many should be in your span of care? Who are the people you will lead, coach, pray for, mentor, challenge, focus, share life with, and help expand your ministry's impact? In how many people can you invest your time and energy without cheating them, your family, and your walk with Christ? If you're anything like me, you're not on the same relational and leadership level as the Son of God, so the number is probably less than twelve.

In my experience, the maximum number of people you can appropriately care for in a ministry role is between five and seven. Any more than that, and somebody's going to be cheated. It might be the members of your team who don't get the attention they deserve. It might be your family. It might be your own ministry influence that will deteriorate over time. You'll spend so much time focusing on others that your passions, including your passion for pursuing Jesus, will suffer.

An appropriate span of care is important for the senior pastor, but it's also important for other staff members, and it's particularly important for volunteers. Volunteers already have the challenge of balancing family and work. Then the church comes along and encourages accountability for a handful of people in a small group—and for another group of people on a ministry team. It can quickly get out of control. Regrettably, I've looked around our ministry too many times and found volunteers responsible for teams of twenty or more people without any additional leadership support.

As a leader of leaders, it's one of your primary responsibilities to ensure that those for whom you are directly responsible also maintain an appropriate span of care. That may mean you need to help them structure their teams to allow for more leadership roles and shared responsibilities. It may mean you need to provide coaching and support to help with leadership recruitment. In any case, you can't let leaders continue trying to care for more and more people. It's bad for leadership, and it's bad for those receiving the poor care associated with an overcommitted leader.

One of my favorite passages in Scripture is Paul's description of the apostles' ministry in Thessalonica: "But we were gentle among you, like a mother caring for her little children. We loved you so much that we were delighted to share with you not only the gospel of God but our lives as well, because you had become so dear to us" (1 Thessalonians 2:7-8).

What a great reminder! Ministry is more than sharing the gospel. It's more than pursuing the vision. It's also about sharing life with our teams and those we're trying to reach for Jesus. It's about spending focused time with *regular companions*, and that can happen only if we limit the number of people who are within our direct span of care.

—Tony

Quality Attracts Quality

If your team is known for high quality in everything it does, then others who appreciate (and can deliver) that level of quality will be attracted to your team. If you print a top-notch church newsletter, then graphic designers or print experts will sit up and take notice. They may want to join your team because they recognize the value you place on quality.

It's also true that talent attracts talent. If Hazel Bermbeck, the church matriarch who can't hold a tune, is your primary singer because of her availability, then you aren't going to attract many singers who can improve the quality of the singing. By avoiding an undesirable, tense conversation with Hazel, you are limiting whom you are able to reach with your service (see Chapter 75, "Embrace the Tough Conversations").

This principle holds true in other areas too. Excellence attracts excellence. Mediocrity attracts mediocrity. Bad attitudes attract people with bad attitudes. Pessimism attracts pessimistic people. Enthusiasm attracts enthusiastic people. Whiners attract others who whine.

Let's not kid ourselves, though. If you are in a new church plant or a small church, you have to work with what you have. In a church with one hundred regular attendees, you feel blessed to have five people who can carry a tune. If your newsletter contains only a few typos, you're happy! So you're probably thinking, "It's easy to advocate this principle when you have several thousand people to choose from."

Let me share some ideas that enabled us to get from one hundred to two hundred, then to five hundred, and then to a thousand and beyond.

Raise the standard. The more your church grows, the higher the expectations of your target will be. People expect more from a church of a hundred and fifty than they do from a church of twenty. They expect more from a church of five hundred than they do from a church of two hundred. As your church grows, you'll need to continually raise the standard for quality and talent. Sometimes you'll need to find the courage to have a tough conversation with an individual to move him or her into a ministry area that is a better fit.

Offer levels of service. As you're raising the standard, you'll also need to offer other opportunities for less experienced or less skilled volunteers to serve. For example, Gloria may not be able to design your newsletter, but can she work on the children's ministry brochures? Darren may not have enough experience to run the sound board in your auditorium, but can he run the sound in your middle school ministry? It's not that those areas are less important. They just have a different scope and smaller audience and therefore may require less skilled volunteers.

Stop doing some things. Sometimes the best way to get something up to the standard you'd like is to just stop doing it for a while. Rather than risking hurt feelings by asking people to step out, take a six-month hiatus. Then re-launch the activity with a new standard of quality and excellence.

Look outside the church. If your church is very small, you may need to look outside the church in order to set the standard for a ministry. When we first planted, we asked people from other churches to run our nurseries for six months in order to set a high standard for safety and security. This gave us time to recruit volunteers. When we launched our band, we asked skilled musicians in the community to play in our band (for free!) for a few months until we could find musicians in the congregation. By thinking outside the box, we were able to set the standard where we wanted it to be.

If you aren't accustomed to raising the standard as your church grows, it will be a difficult transition. It is, however, a worthwhile exercise and will release your church for the next level of ministry.

—Tim

29

There's More to Life Than Doing Church

"While Jesus was having dinner at Matthew's house, many tax collectors and 'sinners' came and ate with him and his disciples"
(MATTHEW 9:10).

This might be the worst thing that could happen in your ministry. You could let your most gifted leaders and ministry volunteers overcommit to ministry inside the church, thereby neglecting their ministry outside the church. There's certainly nothing wrong with attending services, participating in small groups, attending classes, serving in ministry, and participating in other activities that promote relationships with other Christ-followers. All of these activities can help us take steps toward Christ and are good and worthwhile pursuits. My concern, however, is that sometimes we place a higher value on doing things at the church than we do on building relationships with those who don't know Christ.

> Sometimes we place a higher value on doing things at the church than we do on building relationships with those who don't know Christ.

This is probably what aggravates me most about churches. We help people meet Jesus, which is very cool. We help them pursue spiritual maturity, and that's also cool. As they take steps in their faith journey, though, we ask them to get more and more involved in ministry until at some point they eat, sleep, and hang out only with other Christians. That's uncool. While it is true that some Christians are so steeped in the world through their friendships and habits that they must leave it completely for a time in order to establish healthy patterns of behavior, we can't lose sight of the fact that Jesus hung out with sinners.

We conducted an all-church survey not too long ago. The survey confirmed what we've thought for some time: People usually come to a weekend service for the first time because a friend invited them. In fact, we found that eight out of every ten people came to Granger the first time through a friend's invitation. We can do all kinds of direct mail promotions. We can place ads in newspapers. We can rent billboards telling people about our church. Ultimately, though, that exposure in the community is pretty worthless unless people from the church are building relationships with their friends who don't know Jesus.

> Jesus hung out with sinners.

We need to be more intentional about how we're teaching our people to develop relationships outside the church. Yes, they need to learn about serving and the spiritual disciplines, but they also need to understand the importance of hanging out with "sinners." Communicate how important it is for people to connect with family and friends. Encourage them to stay engaged in their careers and to build quality relationships with their peers.

The world desperately needs Christ-followers who are willing to bring a biblical perspective and influence to their work environments. Recently I was chatting with a business leader in our church, and he explained that he continues to have the most problems in his business with the Christians he hires. What would happen if Christ-followers became known in the marketplace for their strong work ethic, their positive attitudes, their loyalty, and their commitment to giving their best efforts every day? Imagine the respect and credibility this would give Christians everywhere!

Don't let your quality leaders and volunteers pull out of their relationships outside the church. People who spend every hour in the church aren't leading others to Christ. It's great to ask your volunteers to connect to ministry, but it's just as important to ask them to stay connected to those who don't know Jesus.

—Tony

Put Down
Put-Downs

"For every kind of beast and bird, of reptile and creature of the sea, is tamed and has been tamed by mankind. But no man can tame the tongue. It is an unruly evil, full of deadly poison"
(JAMES 3:7-8, NEW KING JAMES VERSION).

Back in the mid-1980s, I worked for Del Fehsenfeld Jr. He was the founder of Life Action Ministries and had a white-hot passion for revival and purity in the church. Although he was never able to see his dream come to fruition (he died at the age of forty-two of a brain tumor), he had a huge impact on the church, and the ministry he founded continues today. There is an illustration told about Del that I will never forget.

The story goes like this: A local pastor (we'll call him Bob) stops by at the ministry office to visit with Del. Within a few minutes, Bob begins talking negatively about one church after another and one pastor after another. Del quickly grows tired of it and is ready to give Bob a biblical lesson about gossip. But Del has a better idea when Bob starts bad-mouthing a pastor Del knows. So Del stops the guy in mid-sentence and says, "Could you wait a minute please?" He puts his phone on speaker and dials the number of the pastor that Bob was just talking about. As you can imagine, Bob begins to fidget in his chair and look very nervous.

When the pastor answers the phone, Bob really begins to sweat. Then Del says, "Hey, I've got Bob in my office, and he's been telling me some amazing stuff about you and your ministry. I really believe that gossip is sin, and I didn't want Bob to sin, so I've got him here in my office, and I'm going to let him tell you exactly what he just told me. I'm going to sit here and make sure he doesn't miss anything."

Bob never visited Del again. And I'm guessing that he remembered the lesson: Gossip is never right, and slander is damaging. It hurts people. It destroys reputations. It mortally wounds relationships. It is wrong.

In my family we call these comments put-downs, and they are not allowed. And on volunteer teams, put-downs can undermine everything you are trying to accomplish.

Here are some points to remember:

Put-downs disguised as "put-ups" are still put-downs. My six-year-old, Hunter, and I have had this conversation often. We talk about not disguising put-downs. For example, "Your hair looks really good, for a change." Or "You aren't nearly as fat as you used to be." As adults, we disguise our put-downs even better than that. We use prayer or the spiritual language of "churchese" to cover up our put-downs. "Pray for Joe and Cindy because we all know they have some issues to work through." Or "I hope Jack heard the message today because he really needs it."

Put-downs, even if true, are still put-downs. You could say, "Phil needs our prayers because he's addicted to pornography." It may be completely true, but it is not necessary to say to the entire group. There is no reason to make his recovery more difficult than it would be anyway.

Perpetual put-downers should be put out. Many people slip up and gossip or slander on occasion. James knew that when he reminded us that "no man can tame the tongue." However, if you have people on your team who continually put people down, tear down reputations, or tell your team things it doesn't need to know, you need to deal with them quickly. Give them one or two warnings, and if the put-downs continue, remove them from the team. Nothing will tear down the trust and unity of a team more quickly than someone with a vicious tongue.

Connect these people with a counselor or with an accountability team that can offer them the extra care they need. But don't let their presence tear apart your team.

Leadership is no excuse for put-downs. As the leader of a team, you will inevitably have occasional conversations about an individual's character, behavior, choices, or attitude. This is a necessary part of leading a team. If you are a pastor, you may be involved in counseling situations that will require you to share carefully selected information from those sessions with other pastors on your staff. As you care for the souls of your people, that is right and acceptable. However, don't take it to extremes. Don't share more than is necessary to help the individuals in question.

Teach your team to take the high road in all conversations. Constantly ask, "Do I need to say this? Is it helpful?" Use Philippians 4:8 as a filter for your thoughts and your words. Put down put-downs in your church and on your team.

> "Finally, brothers, whatever is true, whatever is noble, whatever is right, whatever is pure, whatever is lovely, whatever is admirable—if anything is excellent or praiseworthy—think about such things" (Philippians 4:8).

—Tim

31

Expect to Hear, "I'm Not Ready to Serve."

"Moses said to the Lord, 'O Lord, I have never been eloquent, neither in the past nor since you have spoken to your servant. I am slow of speech and tongue...please send someone else to do it' " *(EXODUS 4:10,13).*

Too often it's the people who say, "I'm the person for the job" who are really unprepared to take on ministry. If we fully recognize who we are without Christ, it's appropriate for us to be hesitant to take on ministry because we feel unworthy to serve. None of us is worthy. The challenge is to help people balance appropriate humility while still encouraging them to take their next steps in ministry. We need to recognize that we're hopeless both in life and in our ministry roles without the power of the Holy Spirit.

> Spiritual maturity develops when we demonstrate faith and obedience in situations filled with uncertainty.

By the same token, our relationships with Christ will grow far deeper if we are faithful to his call on our lives. You've probably experienced this in your ministry. How much greater is your understanding of God's Word when you're the one preparing the Bible lesson? How much greater is your faith in God's provision when you're helping to financially resource the church? How much greater is your ability to lead others when you're placed in a leadership role, trusting God to direct your path? Spiritual maturity develops when we demonstrate faith and obedience in situations filled with uncertainty.

Now, of course, some people really *aren't* ready to serve in particular roles. If someone is struggling with a particular sin, you shouldn't invite him or her into a teaching or leadership role that would negatively affect the healing process. On the other hand, no one would be serving in ministry if we were waiting around for people who are without sin. There are times when asking someone to join the team is the best step you could take to help him or her move beyond the sin in his or her life.

> There are times when asking someone to join the team is the best step you could take to help him or her move beyond the sin in his or her life.

That's what happened to Simon Peter. In Luke 5, Simon finds himself second-guessing Jesus. Simon and his partners had spent all night fishing and hadn't caught a thing, but Jesus encouraged the guys to give it one more shot. Though it didn't make sense to them, they followed Jesus' direction and ended up catching so many fish that their nets began to break. After recognizing his own lack of faith, Simon Peter was embarrassed to be in Jesus' presence and stated, "I am a sinful man!" (Luke 5:8b). Even in the face of such a declaration, Jesus asked Simon Peter to leave everything and follow him.

I'm also reminded of young King Uzziah. He was only sixteen years old when the people made him king of Judah after his father's death. Sixteen! Do you remember what you were like at sixteen? My guess is that Uzziah didn't feel exactly ready to lead Judah. Ask Mom for the keys to the family chariot? Maybe. Run a country? Probably not.

Even so, Uzziah was obedient to the call of God. "He did what was right in the eyes of the Lord, just as his father Amaziah had done. He sought God during the days of Zechariah, who instructed him in the fear of God. As long as he sought the Lord, God gave him success" (2 Chronicles 26:4-5).

Obedience may not lead to health and wealth, but I believe it matures our faith. It draws us closer to God and gives us reason for hope in our lives. Encourage people who aren't "ready" for ministry to seek the Lord, to be obedient to his call, and to experience *real* success.

—Tony

Limit Liability

"The heart is deceitful above all things and beyond cure.

Who can understand it?"

(JEREMIAH 17:9).

Awful things happen, even in churches.

We read about them nearly every day. Churches find pedophiles working in their nurseries, embezzlers counting their money, and sexual predators running their singles ministries. Sometimes this news causes us to want to give up on people. "If it's this tough, it just can't be worth it," we think.

People have baggage. Their lives are messy. Even the most well-intentioned new Christians lead lives tangled with years of sin, deceit, wrong choices, and the associated consequences. As Jeremiah lamented, we can't begin to understand the depths of our own hearts. So trying to figure out someone else's seems like a lost cause.

Is it possible to protect ourselves against every unforeseen situation? I doubt it. Can we run a church in a way that makes it impossible for a volunteer or staff member to stumble? I don't think so. We can, however, limit our liability by protecting the areas in which we are most at risk. Here are some ideas:

Children—Most churches have caught on to the necessity of doing background checks on every individual who will come in contact with their children or teenagers. This is no longer optional. It is crucial to protect the kids and the testimony of the church. According to Christian Ministry Resources, "Churches that have screened the alleged perpetrator will be in a better position to reduce their liability risk by showing they acted with reasonable care in the selection of [a] worker."[1] A great source for screening can be found at ChurchStaffing.com.

Brian Davis, children's pastor at Parkcrest Christian Church in Long Beach, California, says, "At the very least every church should have an application process and be checking all applicants against the sexual offender registry. In most states this registry is posted free of charge on their government Web site." Unfortunately, people relocate frequently, so checking only your state's registry is often insufficient. One of the membership benefits of Church Volunteer Central (www.churchvolunteercentral.com) is a full national search of criminal databases and sexual offender registries.

> Training in risk management, plus reproducible forms such as liability waivers, are available at no charge to members of Church Volunteer Central (www.churchvolunteercentral.com).

In addition, make sure that the rooms children occupy are open and roomy and have no hidden corners. Establish policies such as these: "No child will ever be in the bathroom alone with an adult" and "Classrooms don't begin checking children in until there are at least two adults present."

Money—People all around us are under financial stress and, for some, seeing cash is a great temptation. They may fully intend to return the money. They may not even consider the act stealing. They may think they're just *using* the money for a while. For some, taking the church's money is far too easy to justify. Churches must have policies in place to limit their liability. At Granger, no one ever counts the offerings alone. Two or more unrelated (not husband and wife) people are involved in the counting and deposit process. These types of systems should be in place in any ministry in the church that requires people to deal with money.

There are many other areas to consider as well. Suppose a death occurs as a result of a church van accident, and it is later learned that the volunteer driver had a history of driving violations. Or what if all of your volunteer musicians' instruments are stolen during a church mission trip, and the musicians expect the church to replace them? Or you send your small-group leaders to a conference and they total the rental vehicle that the church provided, and now you are looking at spending $25,000 on a wrecked car?

The purpose of this book is not to offer pages of policies. Rather, we encourage you to consider scenarios like the ones we've described and develop appropriate policies and procedures with your team. You can't plan for everything, but you can limit your liability. Remember, stuff happens, and we are in a lawsuit-happy society. So do what you can to limit your church's liability.

—Tim

ENDNOTE

1. ScreenChurchStaff.com, "10 Reasons Why Church Leaders Should Take Screening Seriously."

Give Volunteers Titles

> "What's in a name? That which we call a rose
> By any other name would smell as sweet.
> So Romeo would, were he not Romeo called,
> Retain that dear perfection which he owes
> Without that title. Romeo, doff thy name."
> —*WILLIAM SHAKESPEARE*, ROMEO AND JULIET, *ACT 2, SCENE 2*

Titles are significant. Juliet certainly understood the power of titles in the feud between the Montagues and the Capulets. Titles also have significance in ministry, particularly when they're used for volunteer roles. Though Romeo and Juliet hoped to "doff" them, titles in ministry greatly benefit those who serve...as well as those who are served. Here are some factors to consider when establishing ministry titles for your volunteers:

Use the titles to communicate how much you value the ministry contribution of the lay person and the significance of his or her role. Use titles to say, "You are an important part of our team, and we're counting on you to fulfill your mission."

Use titles to lend credibility to the lay person who is carrying out a particular ministry role. The title should tell those who are being served by the ministry that the church recognizes that person's spiritual maturity and commitment to leading and caring for others. The paid staff doesn't have to do it all; lay people are prepared to handle the ministry responsibility.

Get creative with titles. Go to Fast Company's Web site (www.fastcompany.com) and check out the "job titles of the future." You'll find some creative ways that companies have communicated the unique roles of people in the marketplace. These innovative ideas may inspire you to consider new titles for your volunteers. For example, we call the person responsible for every interaction a newcomer will have outside of the auditorium our Experience Specialist.

Be careful not to offer a role and title too quickly. See Chapter 17, "Choose Proven Leaders," about selecting proven leaders for new leadership roles. It's much easier to *give* someone a new title than it is to take one away.

We've found stewardship campaigns to be one key time we've experienced positive results from giving volunteers titles. When lay people are identified for leadership roles, they are better able to build broad participation from other volunteers. The same principle holds true in other ministry opportunities. You may, for example, identify volunteers who have the potential to become unpaid directors, associates, and lay counselors. This fuels a culture that expects volunteers, rather than staff, to carry the ministry. And that's what allows your church to maximize its growth potential and reach more people for Jesus.

You may not like Shakespeare, but I won't be surprised if I hear you calling out, "O, Elder Ed, Elder Ed! Wherefore art thou, Elder Ed?"

—Tony

Be the "Love Doctor"

Recently I had the same conversation with two different people. They were both upset about the music volume in our services. They couldn't understand why it was so loud. Even though they both addressed the same issue, I felt totally different about the two conversations. With one person, I felt love and support. I felt that he trusted the church and its leaders even though he disagreed with the volume level. I truly sensed that he believed in the church's mission and vision. He was just trying to figure out how the volume level helped us reach more people.

During the other conversation, however, I sensed anger and mistrust. I wasn't sure if the person liked me, the church, or much about life. His feeling about the volume of the music colored his perspective of the entire church. He even said, "We're not sure how long we can stay around if this doesn't change." And, as in every conversation of this nature, he invoked the nameless crowd that stood with him, waiting to see what the leaders would do to address their concerns.

I think a lot of these conversations can be chalked up to getting up on the wrong side of the bed. We all have a bad day occasionally. We have to extend grace to one another.

But if you find yourself in this type of conversation with the same individual again and again, you may be dealing with someone who has a "love problem." It's not the *content* of the concern that indicates a love problem; it's the *way in which* the concern is communicated.

What does it mean to love the church? Does it mean you agree with everything it does? that you never ask questions? that you never get upset about a decision? that you automatically subscribe to every word the pastors speak?

Of course not. The church needs leaders who are both innovative *and* submissive, who are initiators *and* followers, who have their own ideas about how to accomplish the mission *and* are radically committed to the direction of the church leadership, leaders who know when and how to challenge a decision *and* intuitively know the right time to rally the troops behind the cause.

When you are selecting volunteers for your team, it is important to make sure they love the church. This love manifests itself differently based on their maturity level and tenure at the church:

Pre-Christians or Those Who Are Brand-New to the Church—*Honeymoon* is the best way to describe their experience. They invite all of their friends and acquaintances to church. Everything about the church is new and exciting to them. They begin to take steps in their faith, and their stories are compelling and contagious! You'll want to connect this group of volunteers in meaningful ministry right away, but make sure they don't get overcommitted.

Those Who Have Been Around for a While—As in marriage, when you've become "seasoned" in the church, your love begins to be expressed differently. *Committed* is the word to describe this group. These people truly love the church, but they realize it isn't perfect. But that's OK for them. They give their time and energy to make it better. They are no longer *consumers*; they have become *contributors*. They realize church is not just for them, and they want to help make an impact on others. They show their love through their ministry, their giving, and their words. When they are confused about a decision or direction, they talk to you about it. You feel their love and support while they express their concern. You sense that, even if they don't agree with you, they'll still be on the team, pulling as hard as they can to accomplish the mission.

So sometimes you have to play the role of "love doctor." If people in your church have a love problem, work hard to recast the vision. Help them renew their love. Make sure they are seeing stories of life change. You might need to have a heart-to-heart talk with them. But until you are sure, don't put them in positions of leadership or influence.

—Tim

Respect Their Time

I t's one thing to arrive on time for a meeting at work only to find that others are late and no agenda has been prepared. It's frustrating, but you're still getting paid in spite of someone else's ineptitude. It's quite another thing for a volunteer to experience this. Volunteers may already be working forty- and fifty-hour weeks; they may be moms who have arranged baby-sitters for their kids. When you're not prepared for these people, you're essentially saying, "Your time doesn't matter." That's the quickest way to turn people off from serving on your ministry team.

It's so important to maintain integrity with time. We live in a fast-paced culture, running constantly between our families and careers. At Granger, lack of time is the most common reason people won't join a small group or step into ministry. We've heard people say it again and again, and we've documented it in surveys as well: People are too busy.

With that in mind, we need to respect their time, and that can begin with the small stuff:

Start and end meetings on time. Plan meetings so that you'll use the time you have together wisely. Don't try to pack too much into your meetings. In addition to addressing the decisions that need to be made, allow time for people to share what's happening in their lives.

Prepare. You don't need a printed agenda for every gathering, but you should go into every meeting with an action plan and a knowledge of what outcomes are desired. Preparation gives focus to conversations and improves the chances for a successful gathering.

Eliminate needless meetings. Do you really need to get the whole team together, or could you just process everything in a side conversation with one or two people from the team? Does the issue at hand require everyone's input? Meet only if you have something worthy of discussion. I love this line from Patrick Lencioni's leadership fable *The Five Dysfunctions of a Team*: "Let me assure you that from now on, every staff meeting we have will be loaded with conflict. And they won't be boring. And if there is nothing worth debating, then we won't have a meeting."[1] Of course, it's important to pursue only healthy debate, as we describe in Chapter 47, "Agree to Agree."

Return calls and e-mail messages. Respond promptly to people when they contact you. If you continually find yourself stretched for time to answer people by phone or e-mail, that may be a good indication that you have too many people in your span of care. (See Chapter 27, "Limit Your Span of Care.")

Keep projects moving. Good project management is one of the keys to successful volunteer leadership. Provide schedules. Make sure all the team members know their assignments. Monitor progress in checkpoint conversations. Don't let the team become discouraged because it's not seeing any momentum.

When volunteers sense that their time is not being used wisely, they check out. And who could blame them? You're competing with everything else that they could be doing with their time—hanging out with their kids, playing golf, making money. Respect your volunteers, therefore, by respecting their time.

—Tony

ENDNOTE

1. Patrick Lencioni, *The Five Dysfunctions of a Team* (San Francisco, CA: Jossey-Bass, 2002), 103.

You Can't Fix Everyone

"Is not wisdom found among the aged?
Does not long life bring understanding?"
(JOB 12:12).

It's said that people get wiser as they get older. I've met some exceptions to that rule, but all in all, I think it is true. It is definitely true with me. I'm now in my mid-thirties, and I know that I'm much wiser than I was even five or ten years ago.

Here's one example: I used to think I could fix people. I thought if I had enough time and focus, I could talk them into wellness. I could set them on the right path and get them going in the right direction. I think I really believed that people make wrong choices because they lack information.

Of course, I was wrong. First of all, there is the theological truth that it is Jesus, not I or anyone else, who changes hearts. Second, there are some people who just can't be fixed quickly. They have spent years or even decades making wrong choices and developing bad habits, and—although Jesus can and will change their hearts—they still have a lot of baggage to sort through.

Since we are in the business of introducing broken people to Christ and helping them get on a path toward wholeness, one natural byproduct is that the people on our teams are at various levels of brokenness (including ourselves and all our leaders!). But sometimes this brokenness is beyond the team's ability to deal with, and it begins to hurt the team.

Here are some signs that a person on your team is disabling the group:

- Conversations during your "team time" are monopolized by one individual.

- The individual talks about his problems at every opportunity. He shows no interest in the issues of others. When others share, he responds with an "I can top that" story of his own.
- She is "leechlike." Others feel the energy being sucked out of them when she is around.
- Your group's attendance and involvement become sporadic. Your team may no longer be enjoyable because of one person. Without changes, you may lose your team.
- He is facing issues in his life that neither you nor your team members have been trained to deal with.
- He is a constant whiner or gossip, and this is dragging down the team. (See Chapter 30, "Put Down Put-Downs.")

Entire books have been written on this subject, so we won't try to solve the issue in five hundred words or less. The bottom line is that you need to have an "outplacement" system for those on your teams who need more specialized help. I've heard of some churches that actually call those individuals ECRs ("Extra Care Required"), and they have an ECR plan in place that all the leaders are aware of. When someone fits the ECR profile, they follow certain steps to promote the health of the individual and that of the team.

As Christians, we tend to convince ourselves that we should keep individuals on the team as long as possible. We often don't see the damage this causes until we see the situation in hindsight. It seems uncaring to kick a person off the team because he has big problems. "Who am I to rate his problem as more complicated than my own?" we ask ourselves. And yet the reason we need to handle it is because that individual will not get the help he needs in the context of a healthy team. Yes, he needs friendships. Yes, he needs unconditional love. But he also needs specialized care. He needs someone who can help him through the "stuff" of his life.

For the sake of your volunteers, accept the fact that you can't fix everyone. This frees you to be a stronger leader, to build better teams, and to introduce people to environments in which they can really be helped. It also makes you look wise beyond your years, and we could all use that help.

—Tim

37

Creativity Doesn't Just Happen

"In the beginning God created the heavens and the earth"
(GENESIS 1:1).

There it is. In the very first words of Scripture, we're reminded that we serve a creative God. And since man is created in God's image, it's no wonder our culture is filled with artistic expressions that reflect God's passion for creativity. We tend, however, to think of creative expression only in terms of the arts. Creativity can be expressed in many other ways in the church besides music, drama, and media. When we see it expressed in areas such as leadership, systems, communications, and care, for example, that's where breakthrough ministry strategies happen to help the church increase its capacity to reach more people for Jesus.

Add gifted people to the team. A ministry that embraces creativity and innovation begins with a leader who is willing to empower other leaders around him or her to generate new ideas. It takes a leader who is humble, someone who is confident enough in his or her own leadership role that he or she can bring others along who are capable of generating the next big thought.

This attribute was a characteristic of the greatest leader of all time. "Though he was God, he did not demand and cling to his rights as God. He made himself nothing; he took the humble position of a slave and appeared in human form" (Philippians 2:6-7, NLT). A leader with a spirit of humility is willing to bring deeply talented people to the team—people who, in various capacities, will exceed the giftedness of the leader. When that happens, the level of creativity and innovation is limitless. That's one sign of a true leader of leaders.

Create an environment that fuels innovation. A leader who encourages his or her team to generate the next big thought will also provide fuel for creativity. Do the members of your team have time to create? Do they have time to dream, or are they always focused on completing the next task? Do the office décor and the arrangement of the workspace encourage creativity, or are they uninspiring? Do you encourage your team to be cultural learners by taking in new books, movies, and travel experiences? Do you gather periodically to brainstorm better ways to do what you're doing and consider what God might have in store for your future? The culture of innovation begins with a leader who understands that he or she is responsible for fanning the flames of creativity.

> If a ministry intends to remain culturally relevant through future generations, it must be willing to step into the mire of unformed ideas.

A leader who is committed to unleashing the power of innovation also understands the proper balance between championing efficiency and pushing people into the uneasy chaos of change. It's vital to value excellence and continuous incremental improvements for the systems and strategies that currently work. If you focus only on efficiency, however, you will always do what you've always done. If a ministry intends to remain culturally relevant through future generations, it must be willing to step into the mire of unformed ideas. Finding new strategies sometimes means challenging current strategies. It can be messy. It can be uneasy. But it's in the chaotic world of change that the next big ideas can be found.

Give people the freedom to fail. How do you respond when someone tries a new ministry program or project that doesn't succeed? Do you express disappointment, or do you honor the person who was willing to step into the unknown? I've seen the most creative churches fail. Their teams are filled with failures. Their histories are filled with failed attempts at outreach and discipleship. But in these same ministries, there are also many successes. What makes these churches special is that they celebrate creativity regardless of the results. That encourages an environment in which people take risks. When that happens, teams are more likely to generate the next big thought.

If you want to be a leader of leaders and bring the most out of your volunteers, don't be afraid to add gifted players to the team, create an environment that fuels innovation, and give your people the freedom to fail. Under these conditions, your team is more likely to tap the creative wisdom of the Holy Spirit and develop innovations that will increase the impact of your ministry on your community.

—Tony

38

Never Do Ministry Alone

I began attending Granger in 1993, about a year before I joined the staff. I remember noticing a strange phenomenon on Sunday mornings. A bunch of us would arrive early to set up all the equipment for the services. The first few weeks that I participated, I remember thinking that it seemed rather inefficient. I thought the setup could be done a lot more quickly with fewer people. Sometimes too many people can get in the way.

That's when I first heard one of Granger's values: Never do ministry alone. Always do ministry in teams. Even when it doesn't make sense, do ministry in teams.

It took me a while to buy into that philosophy. I thought of a bunch of reasons it was better to do it by myself:

1. It's easier.
2. It's faster.
3. It takes more work to include others.
4. If there is someone with me, I'm obligated to talk to that person, find out about him or her. If I'm by myself, I can just get the job done.
5. I feel more needed if I'm the only one who knows how to do it. And who doesn't like to feel needed? It's kind of nice when I can stand out because no one else is trained to do my job (even if it is just setting up the coffeepots).

You recognize the fallacy in my thinking, don't you? This chapter isn't new information to anyone. We all know the principle of doing ministry in teams, but how many of us really practice it? I want to challenge you to scrutinize your leadership. Do you do ministry alone? Consider your team. Do people on your team believe it's part of their jobs to find someone to do their tasks with them?

Our job isn't only about performing tasks. It's not only about getting things done. It is to equip people for ministry and to teach and mentor them to become balanced followers of Christ.

When you always have someone with you in ministry, you accomplish so much! You give someone else an opportunity to serve. You build a relationship with an individual, and you make room for real ministry to happen "life-on-life." You make sure that the ministry doesn't rely only on you. You model true mentoring. You communicate that you are secure in your leadership and don't need a role to define you.

So let me challenge you with these questions:

- Do you answer the phones? Don't do it alone.
- Do you copy coloring sheets for the kids? Don't do it alone.
- Do you empty the trash or clean the bathrooms? Take someone with you.
- Do you run a sound board, camera, or video equipment? Show others how they can do it.
- Are you a teacher? Start working with someone as a team-teacher.
- Do you hand out bulletins or greet guests at the front door? Invite someone to join you.
- Do you lead a team? Find an apprentice leader who can take your place.
- Do you serve on the hospital visitation team? Take someone with you.

I think you get the point. Never do ministry alone.

—Tim

39

Simple Policies Simplify Life

"Have fun and be kind to others."
—*A SIMPLY STRATEGIC DAD*

Since the first day I dropped Kayla off for kindergarten, I've had only two simple rules for my kids when I send them off to school. I tell them to have fun, and I encourage them to be kind to others. Both of these rules cover a multitude of possible sins. Having fun suggests that I want the kids to get all they can out of their school experiences. I'm not terribly concerned that they get good grades. I'd rather they focus on doing their best and fully experiencing life. While they do so, I'm also reminding them to be kind to others. That covers many expectations: from showing proper respect to their teachers and others in authority—to how they interact with their schoolmates.

It's possible that my rules will change as they get older, but for now this seems to work. Simple guidelines help focus expectations yet still provide great freedom for them to take on new adventures and get the most out of life.

> Good policies and procedures actually remove barriers and enable volunteers to accomplish more ministry.

Simple policies also work in ministry. The church needs certain guidelines to help everyone stay on course with its mission, vision, and values. Simple policies also empower people to make decisions and carry out ministry efforts without having to wait for decisions from others.

Without any policies or guidelines, people spend a lot of time waiting for someone else to make a decision. May we use the room? May we make the purchase? How can we let others know about our event? How can others join our team? Though having too many rules can create lots of aggravation, a lack of systems can be just as frustrating. Empower volunteers by making decisions on a one-time basis, creating simple guidelines that allow them to carry on ministry.

Here are some examples of simple policies we've implemented to empower volunteers for ministry:

- **Purchasing Guidelines**—We've established a set of guidelines allowing volunteers to make purchases without having to wait for approval from a finance committee or a treasurer. We have set generous dollar limits for staff and volunteers to purchase what they need for ministry programming. As long as they stay within their total ministry budget for the year, they have great flexibility on how they use the financial resources.
- **Reserving Facility Space**—Using a Web-based solution, we've automated the process we use to reserve facility space. Volunteers don't have to go to a facility committee to receive authorization. Instead, from any computer connected to the Internet, they can review room availability, submit a request, define the room setup including special resources needed, and receive e-mail updates on their request.
- **Promotional Requests**—We've created a system in which people fill out a simple form describing the details of the event they're hoping to promote. The completed form then drives all the promotional processes including bulletin ads, platform announcements, PowerPoint slides, and Web updates.

Good policies and procedures actually remove barriers and enable volunteers to accomplish more ministry. These guidelines and systems should make life easier for people. Rather than trying to figure out how to do whatever they want to accomplish or whom they need to ask, volunteers can just take predefined steps and go on with their ministry. When that happens, it will be easier for your volunteers to *have fun and be kind to others*.

—Tony

Don't Drop the Ball

40

I'm not an athlete. Never have been. In fact, the "athlete gene" does not exist in my family tree (apart from my sister, who was a college cheerleader). It completely missed me.

I remember trying to defy the odds. "If I keep trying, maybe I'll become the first athlete in a long history of non-athletes in the Stevens family," I would say to myself. So first I tried the Salvation Army basketball league. Every year, toward the end of the season, we'd be up by forty points and my team would start throwing me the ball in the hope that I could throw it in the general direction of the hoop. And every year, I would end the season without scoring any points.

Later I tried out for the basketball team at my junior high. Then I tried the junior varsity team. I finally settled for being the statistician and manager of the varsity team.

Although I never played on a legitimate team, I learned all the rules of the game of basketball. It's kind of an advanced form of Keep Away. Your team needs to maintain possession of the ball until you get it into the appropriate hoop. If you drop the ball, then the other team will get it and probably score. If you drop the ball enough times, then you lose the game.

When it comes to working with volunteers, we're not just shooting hoops. We aren't just playing Keep Away. We are dealing with precious people who want to make a difference with their lives. It is so important that we don't drop the ball.

There are many ways that churches can drop the ball with their volunteers, but let's consider just a few:

Dropped Ball 1: Ask for volunteers and then don't follow up. This is classic. We appeal for help in the bulletin, several people respond, and they never hear anything. Maybe we changed our minds and decided not to implement the program, or we didn't get the quality or type of sign-ups that we needed, or we just didn't have a system for follow-up. Whatever the case, we must personally follow up with every single person who responded. Otherwise we undermine every effort of the church in the minds of those individuals. We have unintentionally eroded their trust in the church and in our leadership.

Dropped Ball 2: Recruit new volunteers and don't support them. Just throw someone in a class of third-grade boys without any support, and see how long the person lasts. If you want to turn members into ministers for life, you need to support your volunteers well.

Dropped Ball 3: Start a new ministry without adequate leadership. It's not wise to throw a ball up in the air if no one is there to catch it. You might believe that God is going to bring someone along to lead a ministry, but don't confuse faith with stupidity. Perhaps you should trust God to bring the right person along *before* you launch the ministry. If not, you'll be the one to catch the ball. Do this enough times, and you'll find yourself in a constant ball-juggling cycle with absolutely no time to mentor or recruit other leaders.

> Don't confuse faith with stupidity. Perhaps you should trust God to bring the right person along *before* you launch the ministry.

The best advice I have to avoid dropping balls is to employ systems. Develop systems for follow-up, systems for mentoring, systems for recruiting, and systems for support. Without systems you are relying on the strengths, memories, experience, and best judgment of your staff and volunteers. When you do this, balls will get dropped and people will get hurt.

For example, when we do ministry fairs at Granger (see Chapter 23, "Have a Fair"), we won't give a ministry a table for sign-ups unless it already has a plan in place for follow-up. The same is true for requests in the bulletin. We never collect names unless we have a follow-up system in place.

Even if you can't dribble the ball or make baskets, you can become an expert at not dropping the ball.

—Tim

41

The Staff Should Serve the Servants

"Whoever wants to become great among you
must be your servant, and whoever wants to be first
must be your slave—just as the Son of Man did not come to be
served, but to serve, and to give his life as a ransom for many"
(MATTHEW 20:26-28).

Missions efforts are shifting. Rather than sending missionaries to build churches to reach new people groups, we're learning that it's far more effective to equip nationals to spread the gospel to their own people. I recently spent a week in India, where a team from Granger was training church planters in the province of Tamil Nadu. That week, we trained over fifty pastors, most of whom have planted new churches within the last couple of years. Now these pastors are facing a challenge that many churches in the United States also experience. Many of the young churches have grown to a point where they have up to one hundred people gathering each week, but their growth has leveled off. The pastors are looking for strategies that will enable their churches to continue reaching more people for Jesus.

One of the primary focuses of our trip was to help the church planters understand multiplication of leadership. One pastor can disciple and care for only a certain number of people because of limited time and energy. Growing churches understand the importance of releasing these functions to lay leaders. Because we've found this principle to be very effective at Granger, we were training these church planters to help people connect into fellowship, start them on a discipleship track, and then develop a system for identifying people who can serve in ministries, including in leadership roles.

This is a paradigm shift for many pastors. It demands that the pastor shift from doing all the ministry to serving the lay people. It's the kind of leadership Jesus modeled: He established his church by recruiting and equipping the twelve apostles. And it's a necessary step for these churches in India if they are to continue to grow.

At Granger, this leader-as-servant model incorporates the following roles:

> The volunteers do the ministry, and the staff supports the volunteers.

Communicating the Value—We frequently remind both the lay people and the staff that the volunteers do the ministry and the staff supports the volunteers. That important message needs to be repeated often. When people forget this value, they tend to slip back into the "church should serve me" rather than the "I should serve others" mode.

Resourcing the Volunteers—One of the primary roles of a staff leader is to make sure that the lay leaders and their teams have the resources they need for successful ministry programming. That includes allocating resources such as facility space, equipment, leadership, and finances. Often it also means providing assistance with developing volunteer teams.

Completing Administrative Tasks—If volunteers are doing the ministry, staff leaders will need to focus time on administrative responsibilities to support the volunteer teams. That will include tasks such as scheduling, communications, and data processing. If some staff members aren't administratively gifted, it's important to match them up with others who have those skills and passions. Structure and systems are just as critical as the ministry strategy is to encouraging continued church growth.

Casting the Vision—As lay leaders take on significant ministry responsibilities, staff leaders can champion the mission, vision, and values of the church. As you find strong lay leaders to oversee specific ministry programming, the staff will still need to coach the team to stay focused on the overall vision of the church.

Whenever I think of a true servant leader, I reflect on the story of Jesus washing the feet of his twelve disciples. Here was the most powerful leader who has ever existed washing the feet of the men he had asked to join his team. We don't typically think of that image when we consider other leaders, be they in corporate America, the political arena, or even the church itself. Jesus presented a very different image of leadership, one that senior pastors and other staff leaders should embrace and model.

Jesus was a phenomenal leader because he first recognized that he came to serve. That's a great reminder not only for the church planters in India but also for any ministry leader who's committed to the Great Commission and the vision of a growing church. —Tony

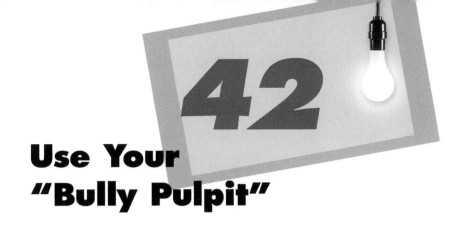

Use Your "Bully Pulpit"

"I suppose my critics will call that preaching,
but I have got such a bully pulpit!"
THEODORE ROOSEVELT

According to the Oxford English Dictionary, a "bully pulpit" is "a public office or position of authority that provides its occupant with an outstanding opportunity to speak out on any issue." The phrase originated with Theodore Roosevelt, who often called the presidency a "bully pulpit." He believed it offered him a terrific platform from which to persuasively advocate his agenda.

In the twenty-first century, who in our world has a better platform from which to persuasively advocate an agenda than pastors? What business or enterprise wouldn't pay a bundle to have the attention of their "customers" the way churches do? Wouldn't Coca-Cola love to have its customers gather every week to hear what it has to say? I'm guessing that Bill Gates would give anything for the opportunity to have the undivided attention of every Microsoft customer each week. Even our president has to fight for attention—it takes a major crisis to get the majority of the citizens of America to tune in.

We can use our weekly service to do more than *just* inspire, although inspiring people is a good thing. We can do more than *just* entertain, even though there is nothing wrong with attracting people and keeping their attention. Why not use our services to motivate people toward action? Why not suggest a "next step" every week?

> Why not suggest
> a "next step"
> every week?

At Granger you'll often hear, "Make your life count. Figure out how God has wired you, and jump into ministry!"

One way we do this is by taking advantage of the bully pulpit. That is, we occasionally design and deliver a four- or five-week series focused on inviting our people to invest their lives in ministry.

A recent example occurred in September 2003, when we launched a fall series called Superheroes. We asked, "Who are the real superheroes in today's world?" Answer: those who are giving their time to make a positive difference in the lives of others. Here are some highlights:

- Most weeks included a live testimony from an individual or couple who had found purpose and relationships through a ministry of the church.
- One week we showed a video that was full of five- to fifteen-second interviews with volunteers explaining why they give time to their ministries.
- We held a Ministry Fair (see Chapter 23) and made sure that every ministry of the church was represented. Because we didn't have enough room in the building, we set up the tables in a tent just outside the main doors of the church.
- We printed a simple flier that listed every ministry of the church, and we included the flier in each weekend's program. We listed a contact person for each ministry.
- We planned orientations and "observer" weekends (see Chapter 12, "Let People Observe") for many of the ministries within days after people expressed interest. We believe that "strike while the iron is hot" is more than a cute axiom.
- During a recap of the series several weeks later, we invited scores of volunteers to stand during each service. After a few words of thanks from the pastor, we cheered and whistled and affirmed them for the way they were investing themselves in the lives of others.

(If you want more ideas to use in your own church, connect to WiredChurches.com to find audio CDs and other resources from the Superheroes series.)

I've seen a lot of leaders who do the "bully" part quite well. In fact, they've mastered the art of using guilt and manipulation to accomplish their goals. I recommend, however, that rather than using your pulpit to bully, you buy into Roosevelt's definition and use your bully pulpit to influence for the good. After all, he had a bear named after him, so he must have been right.

—Tim

43

Seek Ability Over Availability

A few years ago, one of our pastors was working in his office on a Saturday afternoon trying to get caught up from the previous week. A large class had just finished, and a few people were still milling around the building. Lori, our housekeeper, and her volunteer team were in the process of cleaning up and preparing the facility for the services that would take place later that evening.

While the housekeeping team was working, a woman stopped Lori to ask if one of the pastors was still in the building because she needed some counseling. Lori made her way back to the office area, found a pastor, and asked him to come out and talk with the woman.

He was more than willing to chat with her, so he went out to meet her and see if he could help her out. When he approached, the woman took one look at him and asked, "Are you the only pastor left?"

You guessed it. That pastor was me. The woman was obviously a little disappointed that I wasn't one of the more experienced pastors who also work at our church.

She knew that when it comes to counseling, ability is much more important than availability. Frankly, I couldn't blame her. My counseling prowess is certainly not the reason they hired me in a leadership role at Granger. Fortunately there are other staff members and volunteers who are much better gifted and trained to serve in that role.

The same principle holds true throughout your ministry. In youth ministry, small-group leadership, teaching, or singing, remember to seek ability over availability. It's better to leave a position vacant for a

> It's better to leave a position vacant for a while than to fill a ministry role with the first person to come along.

while than to fill a ministry role with the first person to come along (unless, of course, that person is a good fit for the role).

Capability counts. This is especially true when you're filling leadership positions. A good example of this was when Moses followed his father-in-law's advice and found leaders to serve as judges. "He chose capable men from all Israel and made them leaders of the people, officials over thousands, hundreds, fifties and tens" (Exodus 18:25). Notice that Moses found *capable* people. More than that, he recognized that their capacity for leadership varied, and some of them ended up leading more people than others.

Placing people in ministry just because they're available will many times cause more problems than it solves. You'll spend more time and energy trying to fix problems and get people back on track. You'll also be doing a disservice to the volunteers who could be helping in ministry areas in which they could better use their gifts and passions. When people serve in areas that match the way God has wired them, they'll love their roles and your ministry will soar.

Help people find positive ministry experiences by remembering to seek ability over availability. People will appreciate it—especially those looking for a good counselor.

—Tony

Easy Access
Is Crucial

"Then Jesus replied, 'Have I not chosen you, the Twelve? Yet one of
you is a devil!' (He meant Judas, the son of Simon Iscariot, who,
though one of the Twelve, was later to betray him)"
(JOHN 6:70-71).

Do you have ministry positions in your church in which non-
Christians may serve? What if people sign up to work with
kids or to serve in your ministry to guests, but after you meet with
them, you discover they have not yet accepted Christ? Do you let them
serve? Are there certain positions in your church that don't require volunteers to have made a decision to follow Christ?

I say, "There must be!" There must be places in your church for
non-Christians to serve. In most cases, you will reach them only
through community and relationship. And what better way to build
relationships with people than by serving side by side with them?

We are living in a relational world. In my opinion, door-to-door
evangelism is dead. Stadium evangelism is mostly ineffective in the
United States. The churches that are effective in bringing people to
Christ are doing so through relationship building. These churches have
figured out how to arrange their small groups so that pre-Christians are
welcome, and they have specific ministry roles that allow *anyone* to
serve, regardless of where they are in their faith journeys.

Here are some examples:

Children's Ministry—You definitely want followers of Christ
teaching the kids and leading the discussion groups, but why can't a
pre-Christian help with check-in, assist students with their activities, or
make photocopies of handouts?

Guest Ministry—Sure, you want your team leaders and guest-services desk volunteers to have wrapped their minds and hearts around the basics of the faith and the mission of the church, but why can't a pre-Christian distribute programs, serve coffee, or help direct traffic in the parking lot?

Outreach—The next time you build a Habitat home, why don't you encourage every Christian to bring an unchurched friend with him or her? When you serve at the homeless shelter, what better way to show other people the love of Christ than by asking them to serve alongside you?

Arts—Those who sing words of praise and adoration should be doing so authentically and therefore should be mature in their faith. But could there be room on a technical team for a pre-Christian? Is it possible that the only way to reach a drummer or bass guitarist is to pull him onto your team so he can rub shoulders with men and women of faith?

Many times people wonder why their churches are full of Christians and why those who haven't yet crossed the line don't feel comfortable in their services. It may be because when non-Christians visit, they sense that there is nothing for them. The preaching is focused on churchy people and is irrelevant to their lives. The music is strange, and only someone who has grown up with it would like it. They can't be in a small group or join a ministry, which means there is absolutely no way they will make any friends. So they are turned off and never come back. As a result, you lose all opportunity to build a potentially life-changing relationship with those individuals.

Allowing non-Christians to serve in your church may be a philosophical shift, but I implore you to wrestle with the idea. Think about the disciples of Jesus. How many of them were Christ-followers when they were called? Is it possible that Judas was given a ministry position (handling the money) by Jesus even though he was not a Christian? Is it also possible that Peter and Andrew were not fully devoted followers of Christ when they left their nets?

Life is too short, and eternity is at stake. There is a world of people who need Jesus, and we're not going to win them by only preaching on Sunday morning or passing out tracts. We must build relationships because that is where life change happens. That is where the love of Jesus can be made real. That is where real people with real problems learn about real hope and find real solutions.

—Tim

Master the Art of Celebration

"They have been a wonderful encouragement to me,
as they have been to you, too.
You must give proper honor to all who serve so well"
(1 CORINTHIANS 16:18, NLT).

I married a very smart woman. Even before we stepped to the altar, Emily was trying to position me for success. She knew, for example, that I tended to miss opportunities for celebration. Knowing our anniversary would be one of those occasions that I could easily forget, she had our wedding date engraved on the inside of my wedding ring. Now I don't have an excuse for forgetting our anniversary and the chance to properly honor my wife.

Some of us are more celebration-challenged than others. We don't know how to give or receive encouragement. We focus on the tasks without celebrating the milestones. We are quicker to point out what's not working than we are to acknowledge what's been successful. Or we wait until there is a success before we share our gratitude for those who have served. Some of us really do have to work at mastering the art of celebration. It just doesn't come naturally.

Over the years, I've tried to discipline myself to improve how I celebrate others. Here are some lessons I've learned:

Find role models who know how to encourage others well. Mark Beeson, our senior pastor, is a great example for me to follow. His life is a celebration of others. If you spend any time around Mark, you quickly learn the value of encouraging those around you. This is a good reason to download weekly messages from people like Mark. You'll not only learn creative ways to communicate biblical truths, but you'll also hear many examples of how to celebrate the people in your church.

Pray for kindness. It's one of the fruits of the Spirit, so there's no question that this is a prayer that God will answer. Don't be surprised, however, if God puts some very unlovely people or circumstances in your life to teach you how to demonstrate more kindness.

Practice celebration. Like anything else, you'll get better at encouraging others if you discipline yourself to practice celebration. In fact, you may have to actually schedule celebration into your calendar. When you begin to see how people respond, you'll begin to look forward to these opportunities.

Vary your approach. People like to receive love and encouragement in different ways. Tell them. Write to them. Send them gifts. Take them out to lunch. Do it publicly. Do it privately. Celebrate when they deserve it. Celebrate when they don't expect it.

Don't expect anything in return. If you do it any other way, it comes across as manipulation. If people ask, "What do you want now?" that might be a sign that you're using encouragement to get something rather than to build others up.

Quality celebrations are a key to good leadership. Make it a priority to learn how to improve how you're honoring those on your team.

—Tony

46

Volunteers Are Sinners Too

"But Jesus bent down and started to write on the ground
with his finger. When they kept questioning him,
he straightened up and said to them, 'If any one of you is without
sin, let him be the first to throw a stone at her' "
(JOHN 8:6b-7).

ere are some questions to wrestle with:

- Is it OK to have a volunteer on your team who you know is living in sin?
- Are some sins "little" and other sins "big"? If Jesus sees all of our sins in the same way, should we as leaders also see them that way?
- Should we ignore "little" sins, such as lying, but kick people off the team for the "big" sins, such as marital infidelity?
- If you discover that a volunteer is living in sin, how should you approach him or her? What, if anything, should you say to the rest of the team? If it's one of the "big" sins, should you tell the whole church?

It would be nice if I could give you some easy answers to these questions, but short, trite answers won't suffice. I do believe that how you choose to handle sin will affect your ministry. We are in the life-transformation business. That, by definition, means we are helping people take steps away from their formerly sin-filled lives. So in the church, we will be surrounded by sinners who are either living in sin, leaving their sin, or loving their sin.

How the church responds will influence how successfully believers are able to recover from the crippling choices of their past. If, when we find out about sin, we automatically tear the person out of the only God-honoring relationships he or she has, then we may do more harm than good. Although there are no easy answers, I believe we can apply some filters to help in these tough situations:

Christ Filter—As we discuss in Chapter 44, "Easy Access Is Crucial," some ministry positions should be available to those who have not yet accepted Christ. Then, when volunteers sin, we must apply the "Christ filter." If they are pre-Christians, we should have different expectations of them. Giving up certain lifestyles or curbing profanity is not their next step. They should continue to attend services and deepen Christ-honoring relationships so that they will eventually meet Christ.

> In the church, we will be surrounded by sinners who are either living in sin, leaving their sin, or loving their sin.

Maturity Filter—In your church there are brand-new Christians who are discovering new ways to follow Christ every day. You also have seasoned Christians whose level of education has far exceeded their level of obedience. You must apply a higher standard to the seasoned believers among you.

Leadership Filter—A leader is held to a higher standard (Luke 12:48b). You may have someone on your greeter team who is struggling with purity in his or her dating relationships. The best way for that individual to take the next step is to be in relationship with other believers in the context of a church. However, if you find the leader of that team involved in such sins, then you probably will want to have the individual step down from leadership while he or she is getting help and counseling.

Impact Filter—What is the impact of the sin? Is it primarily personal, or is it affecting others? Even though all sin is deadly and erodes relationships and trust, there are some sins that are far more damaging. For example, cheating on your spouse would have a far greater impact than cheating on your taxes. The impact of the sin affects the "how" and "when" you will address it.

Intent Filter—Some people have fallen into patterns of behavior that have become second nature to them. Those people need education and help. Others are very aware of the pathway to their sins, but they choose to return to it again and again (Proverbs 26:11). The filter of intent is very important when determining a response.

Scope Filter—This could also be called the "position filter" or "influence filter" (James 3:1). You may have two people in leadership who have far different levels of influence. For example, a small-group leader has influence over his or her small group. On the other hand, a leader in your band may have influence over the entire church! This will affect how you deal with the sin.

It is crucial not to prescribe pat responses or procedures for "processing" sin when it surfaces. Each situation must be handled prayerfully, delicately, and individually. And, in some cases, the best response is no response except to continue loving the people who have sinned, building relationships with them, and putting them in situations that will encourage them to grow in their faith and understanding of the Scriptures. Remember, none of us is without sin.

—Tim

Agree
to Agree

"I appeal to you, brothers, in the name of our Lord Jesus Christ, that all
of you agree with one another so that there may be no divisions among
you and that you may be perfectly united in mind and thought"
(1 CORINTHIANS 1:10).

I recently had a conversation with a pastor whose church needed to fill a position on its leadership board. Rather than finding someone who was fully committed to the mutually agreed-upon mission, vision, and values, some in the church thought it would be healthy to include someone with differing opinions. Though they weren't dissatisfied with the direction of the church, they thought it would be helpful to balance the current leaders with someone who would promote a different ministry strategy. In a sense they were hoping to create a system of checks and balances so the leadership power wasn't saturated with one ministry strategy.

That type of thinking may be appropriate in the political world, but it's not biblical for developing leadership teams in the church. The passage referenced above is one of many scriptural examples that encourage church leaders to eliminate divisions and be "united in mind and thought." Because of that, we should be looking for prospective leaders who are fully aligned with the current leadership team rather than those who might offer dissenting viewpoints.

The wisdom of this principle is evident as a team operates together on a regular basis. It's not helpful for leadership teams to be filled with dissension. It's OK for team members to challenge current thinking and suggest new approaches. In fact, creating an open environment that allows members to confront one another on tough topics is actually a sign of health. It's not acceptable, however, for unresolved disagreements to remain.

With that in mind, here are some decision-making strategies to help your team move toward biblical unity:

Avoid voting. Anytime you take a vote, you'll end up with winners and losers. Remember, the biblical model is to reach a place where there is no division, and that's not possible when you have people on two sides of a vote. There are ways to build accountability into your system without voting. If you are modeling the early church in the book of Acts, you may decide it's actually more biblical to throw dice to make decisions than it is to vote (see Acts 1:26). I don't recommend this method, but it would be kind of funny to see everyone pull out a pair of dice for the next big decision facing your church.

Avoid compromise. When you use compromise as a method of reaching a decision, you're giving the weakest links on the team the most prominent position because they're pulling the rest of the team in their direction. These people could be well-meaning but misinformed. Or they could be new Christians who aren't spiritually mature. Or they could be individuals filled with spite and motivated by bitterness and revenge. Whatever the case, the weakest person could be pulling the rest of the team away from what ultimately could be the best decision. If 90 percent of the group members agree on a particular decision, they shouldn't compromise to get full agreement from the last 10 percent unless that compromise actually generates a better result.

> Open dialogue and debate generate better ideas, and unified teams generate better results.

Avoid agreeing to disagree. Disagreement still suggests a lack of unity. Though your team may not reach full agreement on every issue (it should on most), everyone should leave every gathering ready to support the final decision. Each member should be fully prepared to share and champion the decision. If that isn't the case, the issue requires further dialogue or, in the worst-case scenario, you may need to change your team.

Avoid unilateral decisions. One of the things I've appreciated most about being a part of the senior management team at Granger is the fact that there are never any unilateral decisions. On any matters of significance, our team discusses the options and reaches a decision together. I can't remember the last time our senior or executive pastor made a major decision on his own without consulting the rest of the team. Because of that, healthy decision making is being modeled for the entire ministry.

If you want to create an environment that promotes new ideas, allows for honest feedback, and preserves the unity of the team, you'll need to *learn how to debate, then agree to agree*. Jim Collins described it this way in his book *Good to Great*: "You need executives, on the one hand, who argue and debate—sometimes violently—in pursuit of the best answers, yet, on the other hand, who unify fully behind a decision, regardless of parochial interests."[1] Open dialogue and debate generate better ideas, and unified teams generate better results.

If you are truly committed to biblical leadership principles, you will agree to agree. This strategy needs to be championed throughout the ministry for both staff and volunteer teams. Effective ministry begins with clear vision, and clear vision begins with unified leadership.

—Tony

ENDNOTE

1.   Jim Collins, *Good to Great* (New York: HarperCollins, 2001), 60.

48
Don't Underestimate the Soft Sell

Soft sell. It may be a marketing term, but it works in the church. Even when you aren't specifically casting a vision that will encourage people to invest their lives in ministry, you need to show the benefits. Even when you aren't talking about serving and making a difference, figure out ways to show how people are making a difference. Even when it's not the Sunday to recognize volunteers, work affirmation into your message.

This is crucial to creating a church culture in which volunteering is normal, the members are the ministers, and people feel valued for the roles they fill and the parts they play.

Videos—Show videos of happy volunteers even when you aren't asking people to sign up for anything. We do this all the time, typically with a three- or four-minute video at the end of the service. We'll highlight a recent event and include images of the volunteers who pulled it off. Whether it's a video about a women's retreat, camp adventure, or our spring campus workday, we will spotlight huge numbers of volunteers making a difference with their lives.

If you don't do anything else with video in your church, do two things. First, show the faces of happy kids in your children's ministry who are being cared for by qualified adults. Second, show the faces of happy volunteers making ministry happen around (and through) your church. This will inspire and affirm those who are currently serving and motivate those who aren't yet serving but want to make a difference with their lives.

Stories—Work stories about volunteers into your messages. When you're talking about faithfulness, use a story about a volunteer in your church whose faithfulness has inspired you. When you're talking about sacrifice, talk about the women who gave up a whole week to cook food for the kids at camp. When you're talking about family relationships, talk about the family who spent part of its Christmas vacation delivering food to the less fortunate. When you're talking about the creativity of God, give examples of musicians, artists, designers, and architects who are using their skills in the church.

Include stories like these in your newsletter or on your Web site. Ask some of your volunteers to write about why they serve, how their service affects their lives, and what they receive through serving.

The soft sell works. And when you're delivering the yearly or biannual "make a difference with your life" message, it will go a whole lot better if you've been paving the way with the soft sell.

—Tim

"Good Enough" Isn't Good Enough

"So whether you eat or drink or whatever you do,
do it all for the glory of God"
(1 CORINTHIANS 10:31).

'm increasingly convinced that the church is the only place in America where "good enough" has become the accepted mode of operation. Everywhere else I go—restaurants, theaters, sporting events, bookstores—I see a focus on giving people a "Wow!" experience. The goal is to *exceed* customer expectations. When I walk into Barnes & Noble or Starbucks or Krispy Kreme, I don't see any indication that they're satisfied with providing an experience that's "good enough."

It's funny, but you'd think that churches would be setting the standard for exceeding expectations and providing the best guest experiences possible. After all, we're not just selling books or coffee or doughnuts, we're trying to introduce people to Jesus Christ. We're offering people forgiveness, hope, and new life in Jesus. You would think we'd be so compelled by that mission that we'd always be putting our best foot forward.

You would also expect churches to always strive for excellence because of passages such as 1 Corinthians 10:31 that encourage us to "do it all for the glory of God" and Colossians 3:17: "Whatever you do, whether in word or deed, do it all in the name of the Lord Jesus." Neither of these passages suggests that "good enough" is sufficient in the church.

I think one reason we settle for "good enough" in the church is that we try to do too much. That forces us to stretch our time, energy, resources, and volunteers too thin instead of focusing on doing just a few things very well. Second, I think we assume that because we use volunteers, it's OK for the church experience to be sub par. That doesn't have to be the case. Volunteers can deliver great experiences if you help them find places to serve that match their gifts, interests, temperaments, and abilities. As we discuss in Chapter 28, "Quality Attracts Quality," you'll also find that volunteers who are committed to quality will attract more volunteers with the same commitment. On the other hand, if you choose to maintain low expectations, you'll continue to get lower results.

Are you just getting by, or are you glorifying God? Regardless of your church's size or culture, maintain high expectations of the quality of ministry programs your teams deliver. Just because it's free help doesn't mean it has to be mediocre help. People want to serve where they know they are contributing to a win, and one way to generate a win is to exceed the expectations of those who are being served by your ministries. It honors God when people say "Wow!"

—Tony

> At Granger we believe that a positive weekend experience is critical in order for people to be receptive to the gospel message. We want people to say "Wow!" because of their interactions with volunteers—from the parking lot to the children's ministry center to the worship area.
>
> Mark Waltz, Granger's Pastor of Connections, has designed training for our volunteers to help them leave a great first impression with our guests. That training is also available to other churches through one-day workshops on Granger's campus. Check out the "First Impressions Last" workshops by visiting WiredChurches.com. Mark's book, *First Impressions: Creating Wow Experiences in Your Church* (Group Publishing, 2005), also shares many of the principles we've implemented to create "Wow!" experiences for our guests.

50

Leverage the Platform for the "Big Asks"

I know what you're thinking: "Tony said in Chapter 1 not to ask for help, and now Tim is telling us to use the platform to ask for help. These guys need to talk to each other." Am I right?

The chapter titled "Don't Ask for Help" is about *how* to present a need. It's not about the need; it's about the person. It's not about a job to do; it's about helping people find their purpose and significance. But this chapter focuses on *when* to do that from the platform and *how* that might look.

Rule 1: Less is better than more. Platform announcements or "asks" are your trump card, to be played only occasionally. It's not a card to pull out every week. The more you play this card, the less effective it becomes. The less you use it, the more effective it is. Be very strategic about the areas for which you cast vision in a given season. Meet with your senior leadership, and figure this out for the upcoming year. Don't make a "big ask" more than once a quarter.

Rule 2: New is better than old. People love to get in on the ground floor. They love to be the pioneers. They love to build something from the floor up. It's less exciting to be involved in something that's been around for a while. So leverage the platform to cast vision for new ministries. Perhaps you will use it to launch a new service, and you need thirty adults to step up and use their gifts to make it successful. Perhaps it's a new children's department, a new ministry, a new band, or an outreach to the inner city. New is always better than old.

Rule 3: Vacant is better than forced. When you are sharing the vision for a specific ministry, always tie it to the way God has wired people. Here's a good example: "Some of you were created by God to make a difference in the lives of children. You feel as if you're soaring when you're teaching or caring for children. We're looking for thirty people with your wiring to help launch this new class." Here's a bad example: "We need thirty people who would be willing to make the sacrifice to work with kids for a few months to get this off the ground..." It's much better to leave a role vacant than to fill it with someone who is forced into a ministry position that doesn't fit. (See Chapter 21, "Learn How People Are Wired.")

Rule 4: Outcomes are better than inputs. When you're casting vision, talk more about the results of the ministry and less about the work required. Talk about the lives that will change, the relationships that will be built, and the ministry that will happen. Don't focus too much on the specifics of the job. That will come later, during the observation or training phases.

Used sparingly and correctly, the platform can be an effective tool for communicating the vision that people need to make a difference. Used wrongly, it's merely a time-consuming sleep aid.

—Tim

Measure
Ministry

There's no question about it. People are seeking purpose for their lives, and they want to know that their lives count. One way to show people the significance of their service is to measure the impact of your ministry and to share those results regularly. Statistics on their own can be very boring, but statistics in ministry represent changed lives. When they're presented in creative ways, they build momentum and communicate the importance of serving. People are reminded that their ministries are meaningful because they're helping others take their next steps toward Christ.

The best approach to this is to try to measure outcomes rather than activity. Track the measurements that demonstrate how lives have been changed. You might begin by documenting how many people have prayed to receive Christ and how many have been baptized.

But aside from these outward acts, spiritual outcomes can be difficult to determine. You may need to periodically survey your church to measure less tangible developments. The goal is to determine if people are taking steps in a Christ-centered faith journey and showing increasing evidence of the fruits of the Spirit. We recently did this at Granger. Due to the size of our church, we elected to use J. David Schmidt & Associates (www.wiseplanning.net) to design the survey and assist with administration and analysis. We took fifteen minutes out

If you are not in a position to hire an outside consultant to assist with your church surveys, we encourage you to check out *The Gallup Guide* by George Gallup Jr. and D. Michael Lindsay (Group Publishing, 2002). This book includes reproducible surveys and easy-to-follow guidelines to ensure that the information you gather is reliable and accurate.

of a weekend service for people to complete and submit their surveys. Rather than basing decisions and communications on our subjective feelings about the impact of our ministry, we are now able to point to specific facts about whom we are reaching, how people are getting connected into relationships, and how they're taking steps toward spiritual maturity. We know what's working, and we know where we need to focus more prayer and energy.

Once you begin to routinely track outcomes, share them periodically with the ministry teams and the entire church. Communicate them during weekend messages. Use PowerPoint support to demonstrate trends. Share statistics coupled with testimonies to emphasize the life transformation that's taking place. Use these measurements to celebrate what's happening as a result of your ministry.

When measurements are communicated well, people will begin to understand that the time they spend in ministry is having a *real* impact on others. When they're directing traffic in your parking lot on a cold winter day, they'll remember that their ministry counts. When they're stuffing bulletins for the weekend services, they'll remember that their ministry counts. When they're consoling a preschooler who is missing his mom, they'll remember that their ministry counts. When they're rehearsing their vocal part early on Sunday morning when the sun hasn't even come up, they'll remember that their ministry counts.

> Numbers are important because people are important.

Numbers are important because people are important. That's why it's critical to periodically measure the impact of your ministry in people's lives and then celebrate the results together.

—Tony

52

Help Innocent Bystanders

"Bystander dies following North Side bar fight" (San Antonio)
"Seventeen-year-old innocent bystander found dead
after shooting at stadium" (Missouri City)
"Teen Fights for Life After Random Bus Shooting" (San Francisco)

A quick Google search this morning returned 140 news articles about innocent bystanders who had been killed or wounded in American cities in recent days. It happens way too often. An individual is in the wrong place at the wrong time, gets caught in an argument or random act of violence, and dies.

This is a depressing way to start a chapter, but we've all seen innocent bystanders at church (that is, new Christians) get shot down by well-meaning, seasoned saints. When the bullets of immorality, pride, insecurity, gossip, arrogance, and selfishness are coming out of the guns of the "mature" among us, people will get shot, and some will never recover.

It happens when a leader falls. The entire team is devastated by the news. Young believers (or those still seeking) who had looked to their leader as a model of spiritual maturity find that image dashed in a moment. They don't yet have the strength of faith to withstand the storm, and some will give up. They may leave the church in frustration over the hypocrisy, and some may never return.

I've also seen it happen during church "train wrecks." That's what I call it when selfishness and pride invade the entire church, gossip and slander are spread freely, and innocent bystanders are sucked into the vortex of sin and asked to take sides. Everything is muddy, accusations and half-truths are plentiful, and the mission and vision of the church are blurred...or forgotten. The church is left with the accused on one side and the accusers on the other.

Stuck in the middle are the innocent bystanders who just want to go to church and learn about Jesus. They want to worship and grow in their faith, but they keep getting hit by bullets. They want to learn how to be better parents or have stronger marriages, but every time they come to church, someone has a gun out and is shooting across the aisle.

How do we help the innocent bystanders around us? Here are some principles that might help:

Sometimes you can't avoid the bullets. If you're a pastor or if you've been a volunteer leader for very long at all, you've taken bullets that weren't warranted. You've been in firestorms that you didn't start, but being the leader, you've had to deal with them. And sometimes they've been very messy and protracted. Don't beat yourself up just because bullets are flying. Satan is alive, and he thrives on conflict. You should actually be more concerned if things are too peaceful at your church for too long. (It may mean that Satan doesn't see your church as worthy of a battle.)

You may have to get innocent bystanders to safety. Do what you can to safeguard them. Make sure they aren't in meetings where bullets will be flying. There may be times when you'll actually encourage young believers to attend another church for a time. Don't risk damaging their souls while you ride out the storm.

Not every questioned action or criticism is a bullet. It's easy for leaders to get paranoid. If we've been shot at a lot, it's easy to assume that everyone has a gun. There are a lot of people who want to help, so don't put up walls so thick that your family and friends can't get in.

Put someone in charge of triage. When the bullets are flying, ask someone who has gifts of compassion and discernment to watch out for the innocent. Ask that person to follow up with those who have been caught in the crossfire.

Take time to teach about conflict when you're not in conflict. During "peace time" talk to your group or your congregation about how to handle the assaults, threats, and schemes of distracters. A great place to start is by studying how Nehemiah handled Sanballat (Nehemiah 4:1-23; 6:1-19).

Let's do everything we can to stop the bullets. When we can't, let's do everything we can to get the innocent out of the way of the bullets. And when that isn't possible, let's act with humility and grace as we treat the innocent bystanders and pray that their wounds won't be fatal.

Dr. John C. Maxwell gives this advice for confronting those who do everything possible to interfere with the work of the kingdom:

1. Expect distracters.
2. Don't give them the time of day.
3. Trust God to protect you and your reputation.
4. Keep your hands to the plow and don't look back.[1]

—Tim

ENDNOTE

1. John C. Maxwell, *The Maxwell Leadership Bible* (Nashville, TN: Thomas Nelson, Inc., 2002), 582.

It *Is* My Job

Have you ever been in an environment in which people refused to do certain things because those tasks weren't in their ministry descriptions? Have you ever heard someone say, "It's not my job"? Frustrating, isn't it? That baggage from the marketplace is probably the reason I downplay the usefulness of ministry descriptions at Granger. We use them to help us focus on roles that need to be filled and to communicate those roles to prospective staff. After someone joins the team, however, we typically don't talk about the written description again. Instead, the focus is on fulfilling the church's mission and vision. We want people to see the big picture and recognize that a lot that is necessary to the ministry is outside the ministry description.

> A lot that is necessary to the ministry is outside the ministry description.

Having said that, I also want to stress the benefits of outlining your various ministry roles. One of the first steps in developing a volunteer team is to define the roles you need to fill. Start by outlining your ministry structure to define the various teams in your ministry area and their functions. Then list the specific roles for each team. After you've identified the roles, draft a description for each position. Once you've listed all the roles and defined their responsibilities, you can prioritize the positions that need to be filled immediately. Among other things, this process will help you focus your volunteer-recruiting efforts.

Here's a list of items you may want to include in your ministry descriptions:

- a summary of the ministry role
- the relationship between the position and others on the team

(This should answer the questions "Who is my leader or supervisor?" and "Who am I responsible for leading?")

- a list of primary responsibilities
- all the qualifications for the position, which might include personality traits, skills, experience, and spiritual gifts
- minimum requirements including, for example, membership covenants
- a list of what is expected of the person filling the role, including an estimate of the time commitment required

At Granger we've compiled all these ministry job descriptions into our "Ministry Opportunities Manual," a summary of every volunteer role available within the church. We've listed over 225 ministry positions for all kinds of people with all types of spiritual gifts and experiences. You may purchase an electronic download of the manual from *WiredChurches.com.*

The manual helps us connect people with ministry. After they complete our Class 301 to determine their spiritual gifts and other characteristics (see Chapter 21, "Learn How People Are Wired"), a team of trained lay counselors familiar with the manual helps prospective volunteers identify the ministry roles that might fit them best. The counselors are then able to connect people with the ministry leaders because the manual also identifies the contact person for each position.

As your ministry grows, your needs for volunteer positions will change. Make sure you periodically review your ministry descriptions, making additions and deletions as needed. These periodic reviews are also a good opportunity to step back and consider how your ministry teams are structured. They will help you monitor your span of care and determine whether new roles could be assigned to volunteers.

By summarizing each of your ministry positions in writing, you'll have a better understanding of what it will take to raise up the right volunteers for the right roles. When that happens, more and more people will be ready to step up and serve. Then maybe you'll be more likely to hear people say, "It *is* my job."

—Tony

54

Take Care of Those Who Take Care of You

If you grew up in the Midwest, then you've probably heard of detasseling. It's the process of removing the top part of a corn plant, or the tassel, so that the plant cannot pollinate itself. This is done for certain types of corn in order to produce a pure and superior seed.

When I was in high school, I detasseled throughout one summer. Mornings were cold, wet, and muddy. Afternoon temperatures reached 95 degrees or more, but to protect our skin from cuts by corn leaves, we had to wear gloves, hats, long pants, long sleeves, and neck scarves. We would head down endless rows of corn, reaching far above our heads to pull tassels off the plants. By the end of each day, I was scorched, bleeding, sore, and famished. It was miserable.

All the while, our crew supervisors would wait in the clearing and care for us as we reached the end of each row. It might take an hour or more to reach the end of one row before we could turn around and start on the next one. Our supervisors would meet us, provide water, and offer moral support. They would also answer any questions we might have (it was complicated, you know).

They took care of us.

In the business world, it is the companies that take the best care of their employees that are given high marks and voted the best places to work. How much more, then, should we care for volunteers—those who are giving their time? You are probably already doing much in this area that should be celebrated. But all of us can do more.

Here are some examples from Granger that show some specific ways we've placed a high priority on caring for the volunteers:

Building Design—As we plan new facilities, we consider that the ministry will be undertaken by volunteers, and we make the necessary adjustments. For example, we used larger trusses than necessary so that our volunteer lighting team wouldn't have to bend over or crawl when working from the catwalks. We built a greenroom for our volunteer artists. We are currently designing a room to care for our First Impressions team during services.

Volunteer Workspace—Although we don't have nearly enough, we provide workstations for volunteers who help with ministry tasks during the week.

Computers and Equipment—We make sure that volunteers who need them have access to copiers, telephones, computers, two-way radios, and other equipment.

Training—When we ask a volunteer to fulfill a role, we make sure we provide the necessary training resources (see Chapter 74, "Just-in-Time Training"). It's possible to provide centralized training that doesn't cost a lot of money. Check into the cost-effective training offered by Church Communication Network (www.ccn.tv).

Food—When we have meetings or training events, we offer food whenever possible. This helps to reduce the formality of the event and gives people an excuse to come early or stay late to build relationships.

We're not pulling tassels off corn. We're not making widgets or flipping hamburgers. We're not convincing people to work with us by paying them money or offering fringe benefits. We're dealing with unpaid servants of God who want to make a difference with their lives. Let's do everything we can to take great care of them!

—Tim

55

Not All Volunteers Are Created Equal

One of the things I enjoy most about our church is the fact that there's a place for everyone. No matter what your passion or skill is, there's a place for you to give your time and energy to serve Jesus by serving others. Even within each ministry, there are places for people with very unique capacities. In fact, we try to develop three somewhat unique roles on each ministry team. None of them is more important than the others, but every team needs people in each of these roles.

Doing Ministry—First you have volunteers who are "doing" ministry. An example at Granger of people serving in this capacity are all the volunteers involved in our care ministries. We have volunteers who are active with hospital visits, prayer, and helping people who are homebound. In a church of several thousand people, these ministries are always on the go. There is always someone who is hurting or lonely or searching for answers and is looking for support from our community care ministries. Instead of hiring more and more pastors to handle these ministries, we've empowered volunteers who are gifted and passionate about serving others in this way. When we think of volunteers, we think first of people like the ones on our community care team who are actively *doing* ministry.

Supporting Ministry—In addition to the "doers," there are lots of people in your church who love to work behind the scenes. These are the volunteers who are supporting ministry. They may very well be the true servants. They aren't highly visible, so they don't get a lot of public recognition. That's OK, though, because these people typically are motivated more by the satisfaction of serving others than by public recognition (though that doesn't mean they don't need a pat on the back every so often). At Granger, an example of volunteers who support our care ministries is the team of people who type out all the prayer requests each week. This team meets on Monday mornings to compile all the prayer requests we've received during the weekend services. They then type them up and e-mail them to everyone on our prayer team. Many churches pay people for these support roles. In reality, though, if we filled these roles with staff members, we would be robbing people who love to serve.

Leading Ministry—Finally, there are volunteers who are leading ministry. Again, you don't have to pay people to lead. At Granger we have volunteers leading each of our key community care ministries. Lay people are leading hundreds of volunteers. It's silly to pay people to fill these roles when there are so many people who are more than willing to volunteer their time to help others. Save your salary budget for roles that are more administrative or require specialized skills—the roles that are more difficult to fill with volunteers. It's easier, for example, to find a volunteer who will visit people in the hospital than it is to find a volunteer who will process your accounts payable.

Get creative about how you structure each of your teams, and find unpaid servants who are willing to volunteer by doing, supporting, and leading ministry.

—Tony

56

Eliminate the Lone Rangers

Every ministry at Granger Community Church is connected to someone on the senior management team. There are no exceptions.

I recall a time we were discussing the launch of a new ministry. One lay leader had a burden for a certain ministry, and she wanted the church to embrace it. We all thought it was a good idea. While it wasn't critical to our mission, it still contributed to one of our core purposes. However, there wasn't a natural fit for that ministry in any of our existing departments. No one felt right about adding it to his or her plate. So we decided against it.

Why? Because at Granger there are no "Lone Ranger" ministries. Every ministry has a leader, and that leader is connected to a pastor or director for care and support. In a church with a different structure, you might want to make sure that every ministry is supported by and connected to an elder or deacon. There are many reasons for this:

> It is easy to get lost in the micro-purpose of the ministry and forget the macro-vision of the organization.

Lone Rangers have no one to cry with them. When life is tough, they are all alone. (Yes, even Lone Rangers cry.)

Lone Rangers can easily lose sight of the mission. Since there is no organizational or relational connection to the overall mission of the church, it is easy to get lost in the micro-purpose of the ministry and forget the macro-vision of the organization.

Lone Rangers have no one to celebrate with them. When things go well and lives are being changed, there is no natural way for those stories to be shared with others.

Lone Rangers have no one to challenge them to measure their success. Whatever the ministry, its purpose is not mere existence, but accomplishment. A connection allows evaluation of effectiveness and ideas for improvement.

Lone Rangers have no one to represent them. In discussions about budgets or schedules or staffing, there is no one on the leadership team who has a hand on the pulse of that ministry. Lone Ranger leaders may soon begin to feel devalued and unappreciated.

Lone Rangers are, well, alone. Even if they do have others working with them in their ministries, as a group they are disconnected from the church. They don't have the benefit of being on a team. So let's keep everyone connected, loved, and supported.

After all, it's rarely fun to be alone.

—Tim

Commission Your Leaders

"Publicly commission him with the responsibility of
leading the people. Transfer your authority to him
so the whole community of Israel will obey him"
(NUMBERS 27:19b-20, NLT).

I am a political junkie. I monitor Yahoo to stay current with politics. I religiously watch my favorite Fox News anchors give their spin on what's happening inside the Beltway. I love to debate with family and friends about the strategies and policies that Congress and the president are considering.

Of course, there's no better time for a political junkie than during presidential elections. Starting with the string of announcements from those who have decided to run and extending through the debates, the primaries, and the election itself, it's a truly fascinating process to watch. I can guarantee you that I will be glued to the television on election nights, tracking the electoral votes and monitoring the results.

> This is your chance to build credibility, transfer authority, and help define the role that your new leader will be undertaking.

After elections I enjoy watching the president-elect ramp up his transition team and prepare for his new administration. All of that culminates with the inauguration ceremonies. The inauguration, of course, includes the oath of office, speeches, parades, and lots of parties. While giving the new president a chance to celebrate, the inauguration process also provides a platform for the new leader to be "presidential." It's a chance for the president to build credibility and define the agenda of the new administration.

Though inaugural balls probably wouldn't be helpful in your church context, it is important for you to launch new ministry leaders well. This is your chance to build credibility, transfer authority, and help define the role that your new leader will be undertaking. One way to accomplish this is to commission your leaders. Depending on the role, you may want to hold a formal ceremony to recognize the person's transition to the new leadership position. Other roles may only require an informal announcement to those the person will be leading. In any case, this is your chance to tell the rest of the team, "I fully support this leader, and I'm going to do anything I can to help her succeed."

By taking this step, you're immediately transferring all leadership responsibilities that go with the role. Others will know to go directly to the new person for direction, recruiting, and care issues. That helps your new leader, and it also benefits you because others start going directly to the new leader for the ministry responsibilities that you or someone else from your team used to handle. That frees you up to better focus your ministry energies.

Part of a successful leadership transition is the commissioning process. You may not need to play "Hail to the Chief," but you need to fulfill the responsibility for launching your new leaders well.

—Tony

58

All for One
and One for All

Do you remember this scene from *The Three Musketeers*? With swords drawn, D'Artagnan leads Porthos, Athos, and Aramis in the recitation of their motto "All for one and one for all." The motto summarizes their unity, their common bond, and their willingness to fight and die together.

I'm pretty sure, however, that the idea didn't originate with the musketeers. It seems to me that the concept is biblical. Philippians 2:2 sums it up well: "Then make me truly happy by agreeing wholeheartedly with each other, loving one another, and working together with one heart and purpose" (NLT).

I think the church is at its best when everyone is focused on one mission. Samuel Stone and Samuel Wesley understood this when they wrote the great hymn "The Church's One Foundation" in the nineteenth century.

> The Church's one foundation
> Is Jesus Christ her Lord;
> She is His new creation
> By water and the Word.

They went on in verse two to clarify the church's purpose:

> Her charter of salvation,
> One Lord, one faith, one birth;
> One holy Name she blesses,
> Partakes one holy food,
> And to one hope she presses,
> With every grace endued.

But what happens so often in our twenty-first–century churches? We develop stand-alone ministries. The youth ministry has its own purposes and goals and plans which have absolutely nothing to do with the overall church. The women's ministry is a separate entity. The missions committee has its own projects that have nothing whatsoever to do with the mission of the church. And everyone knows not to mess with the choir!

The church ends up with a federation of sub-ministries. They are all good ministries, but the strength of the whole is decreased because they lack a common vision and purpose. The church crawls along and makes incremental progress without really being able to have a turbocharged impact on the community.

> The secret is knowing what to control tightly and what to control loosely.

It happens so easily, especially if you've followed our advice and empowered the laity for ministry. How can you keep everyone going in a consistent direction if there isn't centralized control? The secret is knowing what to control tightly and what to control loosely.

Here are some keys to keeping all your ministries unified:

Maintain a unified budget and a unified calendar. Everything comes down to time and money. These two issues let you know what your church values. If you allow departmental fund-raising for pet projects, then your leadership will lose control of what gets funded. If your calendar is driven by "first come, first served" rather than by ministry priorities, you might inadvertently create a competitive, rather than a unified, church culture.

Use systems to communicate your church's foundational beliefs. Once you've written a mission statement, a vision for the future, and core values, you have to figure out how to continually get them into the hearts of your people. Even your most faithful volunteers will forget why you exist if you don't constantly communicate this to them. It's not that they're rebellious; it's just too easy to fall back onto what they've known or believed for years. Even the systems you use for scheduling

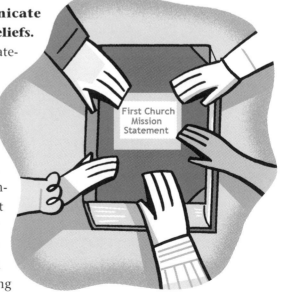

First Church Mission Statement

space in the building or for setting your budget can be great opportunities to restate values and priorities.

Make sure your key leaders see the big picture. You don't want a key leader on your board, elder team, or pastoral staff who is single-minded about his or her ministry area. Someone may have responsibility for missions or youth, but he or she must have the capacity to fly above that and oversee a balanced ministry. If not, then comparisons and turf-guarding will begin to seep into your teams.

At your next leadership meeting, why not put on some musketeer garb, stretch out your swords, and say together, "All for one and one for all!" Then, just before they haul you away to the funny farm, recast the vision for the power and purity of a unified church.

—Tim

Be a "Supermodel"

"Care for the flock of God entrusted to you. Watch over it willingly, not grudgingly—not for what you will get out of it, but because you are eager to serve God. Don't lord it over the people assigned to your care, but lead them by your good example"

(1 PETER 5:2-3, NLT).

One of the keys to servant leadership is modeling appropriate behavior and attitudes to those you're leading. In the passage above, Peter encouraged us to lead by our good example. Paul taught the same principle when he encouraged others to "follow my example, as I follow the example of Christ" (1 Corinthians 11:1). It's why Paul didn't shrink from urging others to "imitate me" (1 Corinthians 4:16).

Here are a handful of critical ways that you, as a leader of volunteers in ministry, can mentor others and establish positive discipleship relationships:

Model *team*. Don't do it on your own. If you're traveling, take someone with you. If you're tackling a big project, find others to help. Take time to meet regularly with teammates to talk about your next steps in ministry and in your own spiritual journey. I can't recall a time at Granger that a decision came down from the senior pastor without any input from the rest of the team. Instead, the senior management team provides organizational and spiritual leadership for the ministry. It's not something that the senior pastor does on his own. It's a lot easier to implement a team-based approach when it's being modeled from the top.

Model *serving*. No, you shouldn't do everything. It's problematic when the pastor is the only person who does ministry in the church.

The pastor and other paid staff, however, should model serving for all the volunteers. Most people are raising families and working in other jobs before they begin serving in their ministry roles. The paid staff should model that as well by serving on the front lines in addition to fulfilling their paid ministry roles. It inspires others to serve when they see their leaders get in the trenches from time to time.

Model *balance*. People need to see good examples of balancing family, work, social, recreational, and spiritual lives. Too many members of leadership in growing churches are burned out because they've failed to make space in their lives for rest and renewal. Ministry is a marathon. Though there may be seasons in which you must sprint, they should be the exception. For starters, begin modeling balance by observing a day of rest each week. (For most of us, Sunday doesn't count!)

> Ministry is
> a marathon.

Model *outreach*. One of the challenges I've experienced in transitioning from the marketplace to full-time ministry is the lack of interaction I have with people who don't yet know Christ. Most of my life is spent at church with staff and volunteers who are already convinced. That means I need to intentionally create opportunities to hang out with "normal" people. Take time to build relationships and share life with people who don't attend your church.

Though not all of us will ever walk the runway, we can all be supermodels if we imitate Christ and model team, serving, balance, and outreach in our leadership roles. Commit to leading others by your good example.

—Tony

60

Don't Steal Talent

Do you want to start a fight? Do you want to quickly develop anger and bitterness among your leaders? Here's how.

Identify the high-capacity, get-it-done volunteers who are serving in other ministries at your church, and aggressively recruit them to work in your area. Say things such as "What would you think about *really* making a difference with your life?" or "If you ever want to stop goofing off and get involved in *real* ministry, let me know!" Tell them about all the perks that volunteers in your area receive, and mention the heavenly blessing of additional time with you. Do this, and you will be sure to invite all the conflict you could hope for.

Obviously, a better course of action is to act like Jesus. Work toward harmony and unity, and stay on mission. Show more concern for the individuals in your ministry than

> Show more concern for the individuals in your ministry than for accomplishing the tasks.

for accomplishing the tasks. Be a team player, and put the interests of others before your own.

It's a balancing act. You *do* want to encourage people to recognize their gifts and use them. You *don't* want to go after people who are already serving just because you have a need. You *do* want to help all the people in your church identify their God-given wiring (see Chapter 21, "Learn How People Are Wired"), and you *do* want them to plug into a ministry that fits. But you *don't* want to interpret everyone's gifting in a way that fits the needs of your own ministry.

Through positive and repeated reinforcement, every ministry in your church can feel connected to the mission. Every ministry can believe that it is important to focus on the vision of the church more than on the task of the individual ministry. Every leader can be more interested in helping people find purpose than in filling empty slots on an organizational chart.

Even when you aren't aggressively recruiting, there will be times when a conversation with a key volunteer in another ministry area will spark your interest. Recently Mark Waltz, one of our pastors, was looking for an individual to fill a ministry role in our church. During his months of praying about this role, he had a conversation with Shelley about her desire to make a bigger difference with her life. She had recently left a lucrative job in order to devote more time to serve at church. As they talked, Mark discovered that her wiring was exactly in line with the role that he needed to fill. There was just one problem: Shelley was the *key* volunteer leader for all major events in our All Stars Children's Ministry.

> Every leader can be more interested in helping people find purpose than in filling empty slots on an organizational chart.

He did the right thing. He quickly went to the director of our children's ministry. Together they agreed that the most important thing to do was to help Shelley find the ministry that would cause her to think, "This is what I was created to do." They also agreed that a shift in roles would take some transition time and that a gain in one area would cause pain in another. They agreed to work together to help each other.

We're all on the same team. Let's start pulling together and show the world how different the church really is.

—Tim

61

Admit Your Weaknesses

"But God made our bodies with many parts,
and he has put each part just where he wants it"
(1 CORINTHIANS 12:18, NLT).

A funny situation occurred a few years ago. We had a transition in one of our pastoral positions, and several of us found ourselves having to pick up additional ministry responsibilities for a time. Among the functions I inherited was our hospital visitation ministry. It's quite comical now when I look back at it. For whatever reason, when God was passing out mercy gifts and characteristics such as compassion and empathy, he completely passed me over. Nevertheless, for a very short time, the administrative pastor was put in charge of caring for sick people.

Now I have to admit, I didn't know there were so many cool benefits to serving in hospital ministry. For example, there's clergy parking. What a perk! Overcrowded parking lots far from the hospital entrance are never an issue, because the clergy get the best parking spots right in the front row. Additionally, you can completely ignore the posted visiting hours. Just wave the credentials, and you're in. Got a hankering for a bedside chat at 8 p.m.? Not a problem when you're a praying pastor. They'll let you walk right in. What a deal!

What I quickly learned, however, is that hospital visitation is more than good parking spots and flexible visiting hours. People actually expect you to provide comfort, care, and hope in their time of pain and fear. They're looking for prayer and counsel. Of course my standard counsel for people who are sick is "Just suck it up and get on with life." Believe it or not, that bit of wisdom isn't helpful for some people when they're lying in a hospital bed waiting to get well.

Fortunately, out of my weakness as a caregiver, a new volunteer ministry was launched at Granger. We found Roxanne, a volunteer in our church who is both familiar with the medical profession and passionate about caring for people in the hospital. She feels called by God to minister to the spiritual and physical needs of others. She is also a gifted leader. It didn't take long at all for Roxanne to recruit and train a team of volunteers to handle the hospital visitation ministry at our church. Now, with very few exceptions, our hospital visits are made by volunteers.

> People don't expect their leaders to be able to do everything. What they do expect is authenticity.

Here's what I've learned through this and other similar experiences: It's not helpful when I try to lead in areas in which I'm not gifted. I not only become discouraged and drained, I also get in the way of others who could minister much more effectively without me. When I operate in my areas of strength, I'm energized, and the church benefits by giving others the opportunity to use their God-given gifts.

People don't expect their leaders to be able to do everything. What they do expect is authenticity. People will respect you more when you're willing to admit your weaknesses. This also allows the church to really value the volunteers who are better gifted to handle various ministry roles. It demonstrates the importance of each person to the body of Christ.

Help people serve in your ministry in ways that best fit how God has wired them. Out of your weakness, others will find meaning and purpose.

Don't look now, but someone wants your parking spot.

—Tony

62

Misalignment Is Bad for Tires and Churches

You've driven a car whose tires are out of alignment, haven't you? You feel as if you're constantly fighting to keep the car on the road. It wears you out and causes tension in your neck and shoulders as your hands keep a constant pressure on the steering wheel. And, all the while, your car is being damaged.

That's a pretty good analogy for what individuals can do to a church if they are "out of alignment" with the direction of the leadership. Let's consider different types of misalignment.

In this example, everyone is heading in the same direction. There is peace and harmony. The church (big arrow) is clear in its direction, and all the leaders or volunteers (small arrows) are heading in the same direction. Conversations center around how to be more effective and how to reach more people, not about nuances of the church constitution or people's likes and dislikes of methods.

Sometimes, though, someone is going in the exact opposite direction of the church and the other leaders or volunteers. It is obvious to everyone. It's not a major deal, though, because the individual is so far off that no one is being influenced. You may have to have a tough conversation with the person, but it won't be hard to convince him that he is not headed in the same direction as the church. And no one else on the team will question your decision.

The most dangerous situation is illustrated here. This is the one that will take your church down. This is the one that you should address quickly! The individual is just slightly off. She isn't advocating doctrines that are diametrically opposed to the church's. She doesn't want to take the church in an *entirely* different direction. She just wants the church to move a few degrees. You've heard her concerns and listened to her thoughts, but she continues to question methods, principles, values, staff motives, and decisions. She isn't even accusing, necessarily. She's just asking questions in a way that tells you what she thinks without leaving herself defenseless if she is cornered. And, of course, every time she has a concern, she makes it clear she is representing unnamed "others" who agree with her.

She never seems happy or satisfied. And you've never done quite enough to please her. This is the person you want to shake and say, "Can't you see all the great stuff that is happening? Don't you notice where God is working?"

This is the person you need to keep on your radar screen. These people may need your loving care and confrontation to bring them back into alignment. If these efforts fail, you may need to "ask them off your team" as quickly as you can (see Chapter 89, "Sometimes You Have to Fire Volunteers"). These people are like poison and will fill a team with doubt, cynicism, fear, and low morale. You may not even notice how far down they have dragged the team until they have left and joy returns.

Of course, this assumes that your church's mission, vision, and values are written and agreed upon. In our membership class, we teach them plainly and ask new members to sign a covenant stating that they will support the church, its beliefs, and our leadership. Then if an alignment conversation is necessary (see Chapter 75, "Embrace the Tough Conversations"), we can point to their signatures on the covenant, showing that they agreed to support the leaders of the church.

A tire that is not aligned can mess up your car. A volunteer who is not aligned can tear apart a team. Both should be fixed.

—Tim

ENDNOTE

Illustrations in this chapter used with the permission of J. David Schmidt & Associates, www.wiseplanning.net.

Leave a Legacy

"Moses was eighty years old and Aaron eighty-three
when they spoke to Pharaoh"
(EXODUS 7:7).

I'm still a pretty young guy, but the thought of growing old already scares me. I tend to think about the group of older men I used to see at the doughnut shop for many years. I'd stop only every few weeks, but I'd see the same group of guys sitting around the same round table. Those of us on the outside used to refer to it as "the table of all knowledge." That's where old men who knew things gathered to discuss all the evils of the world and how to fix everyone else's problems.

Some say that your negative character traits become more pronounced as you age. That's what scares me the most. I can see myself sitting at that same round table forty years from now. That could easily be me sipping my caramel mocha latte, gumming my Krispy Kreme doughnut, and complaining about the weather, the grandkids, and that awful music they've started using during church services. "Can you believe the music they're using these days? Whatever happened to the great songs of the faith from MercyMe, Sixpence None the Richer, and P.O.D.? If there's only one thing we do, we need to get the young people some good Christian music!"

In recent years, however, I've seen some very different examples of how people have chosen to live the second half of their lives. Take Jim and Bev, for example. Both are well into their seventies, but they still faithfully serve in our children's ministry every week. They could have easily stepped aside long ago to give the younger people a chance to lead, but instead they've committed themselves to reaching the next generations. When I grow up, I want to be like Jim and Bev.

There's also Val, a new empty nester. Now that her kids are out of the house, she could have found another job to sock away more money for retirement. Instead, she's committing several hours a week to the global missions efforts of our church. She's organizing teams, helping out in the office, and faithfully launching ministry initiatives that are reaching people on the other side of the world for Jesus. When I grow up, I want to be like Val.

There's some biblical precedence for people like Jim, Bev, and Val. Remember Moses' story? He didn't get his first big gig in ministry until he was eighty years old. That's when God called him to speak before the Pharaoh and lead the Israelites out of Egypt. Granted, Moses lived to be 120 (Deuteronomy 34:7). Nevertheless, he was in the second half of his life when he received his real calling. Think of the many years Moses must have been asking himself, "What's my real purpose in life?" We tend to worry when we have to wait several days or weeks before God answers a prayer. I wonder if Moses was ever anxious during those eighty years when he was waiting for his call.

The point is this: There are people in your church who are still looking for a way to make a difference. For many, entering the second half of life leads to introspection as they consider how they might finish well. Don't forget to tap this valuable resource. You'll find people with time, with great knowledge and experience, and with a renewed commitment to fulfill the calling God has placed on their lives.

I want to leave a legacy that leaves a mark on eternity. That's what I want to do when I grow up.

—Tony

Legalism
Isn't Legal

Legalism is the practice of following a set of rules that you believe to be applicable to *all* people in *all* circumstances at *all* times. Those who follow the rules are righteous. Those who don't are unrighteous.

I used to be a legalist. I loved rules. Rules are easy. When things are black and white, you don't have to think for yourself. All the thinking has already been done. The condition of your heart doesn't matter as long as you obey the rules.

You probably know some Christians who are more concerned with rules than with being real. They care more about the appearance of *doing* right than the authenticity of *being* right. Perhaps, like me, you carry some legalistic baggage.

It's very important that we don't carry legalism into the way we lead our churches. It is crucial that we don't measure an individual's spirituality by a set of predetermined activities or actions. I agree that it's easy to measure people's activity and put them on our "insiders" list based on the number of hours they spend involved in ministry (see Chapter 29, "There's More to Life Than Doing Church"). However, by doing this we risk developing busy Christians rather than fully devoted followers of Christ.

> We risk developing busy Christians rather than fully devoted followers of Christ.

What really counts at your church? When you look at your volunteers, what do you measure? Do you send mixed messages by saying that the Christian life is about "faith without works" while communicating that there are certain activity-based "expectations" of a Christian at your church? Do your volunteers sometimes feel as if they just can't win because, no matter what they do, it's not enough?

At Granger we are trying more and more to measure the extent to which the purposes of God are reflected in an individual's life rather than his or her participation in certain activities or ministries. Here are some questions we ask:

Worship—Is the individual exhibiting a life devoted to God? Is he participating regularly in a corporate expression of worship? (We don't ask if he has perfect attendance at our midweek worship service.)

Fellowship—Is she connected in growing, healthy relationships? Has she identified herself with this local congregation through membership? Although this can happen in small groups, there are other ways to connect as well.

Maturity—Is he taking his next step? Is there evidence of growth in his life? (We don't just ask if he has attended certain classes or memorized the four spiritual laws.)

Evangelism—Does she continually build relationships with the unchurched? Is she inviting and including others? It's not about how many "pagans" she's taken through the "Romans Road" in the last thirty days.

Ministry—Has he discovered how God has wired him, and is he making a difference in other people's lives? Is he doing this in relationship with others? It's not a question of how much time he spends at the church each week.

It gets pretty muddy when you're trying to measure "heart" rather than "activity," but I really believe that doing so reflects the heart of God. I've heard of churches that say, "Every member must be involved in weekly ministry on our campus." Jesus' direction was a little different when he said that the greatest commandment is to love God and the next is to love others. That leaves ministry pretty wide open, doesn't it?

Wouldn't it be great if we taught our believers what is truly important? What if we used a thousand different ways to teach the five purposes of God for the local church and the follower of Christ? Rather than telling our volunteers the activities they need to "do" in order to measure up, what if we continually taught the five purposes and encouraged every believer to measure himself?

Don't get me wrong. Every member should be involved in ministry. But this may not include teaching a Sunday school class or handing out bulletins. It may not even include activities in your building or on your property.

It's pretty exciting when we see our people engaged with the culture. They're putting skin on their faith by giving their time. For example, Don and Bonnie give their time to a local shelter for pregnant teenagers. Elaine and Scott lead our children's ministry in the inner city. Holli teaches young children at the Center for the Homeless. Jim and Mia bought some land and started a retreat center to help pastors find rest and renewal (www.manowe.com).

> It gets pretty muddy when you're trying to measure "heart" rather than "activity," but I really believe that doing so reflects the heart of God.

Let's give our volunteers the tools they need to measure their hearts rather than their levels of activity. Let's make legalism illegal in our churches and instead motivate our volunteers to lead lives driven by the purposes of God.

—Tim

65

You Grow at the Edges

Bill began attending First Church three years ago. A friend from work invited him to visit, and he couldn't believe how much he enjoyed it. At first, he went back a few times somewhat secretly. He didn't want any of his friends to think he was a religious freak. None of his friends attended church, so he knew they would think he was flipping out. But after a while, he began to learn about the Bible and God, and he started to invite some friends to attend with him. He would talk about his experience and then simply say, "Come and see."

After several months, Bill began to make new friends in the church. Some of his old friends had started attending, but he was losing touch with the others. He found that he was filling his time by attending services, serving at the church, and being with his small group one night a week. When his old friends would ask him to go out or see a movie, he usually had to turn them down. Eventually they stopped asking.

> The longer people attend church, the less effective they are with the unchurched or the newly churched.

Now, just three years later, Bill has completely lost touch with all of his old friends. He met Jesus, and his life totally changed. He now spends all of his available time at church or with church people. He has found that his time with other Christians really helps keep him focused on what is right and prevents him from falling into old habits.

Isn't that story typical? The longer people attend church, the less effective they are with the unchurched or the newly churched. It's almost a church rule: "New people reach new people. Old people don't."

We have found at Granger that growth happens on the edges where new people are connecting to the ministry. Those people who are on the edges of your church will most effectively reach others like them. Those who have been around longer and are closer to the core will be less effective with new people. Once you understand this, it will change how you recruit volunteers.

So that you don't face the frustration of volunteer burnout or the disappointment of your "old-timers" not pulling in new people, you need to create systems and opportunities for the new, unconnected people at your church to get involved. They, in turn, will be the ones pulling in their friends.

When you have a social event to plan, don't call your most faithful volunteer, who has been in the church for ten years, to handle the setup. Instead, call the woman who just started attending your church a couple of months ago—the one who stopped to tell you how much she enjoys the church. Ask her to handle the event and recruit anyone she would like to help out. Chances are, she'll pull in volunteers that you have never met and would never have reached. She will grab people who aren't burned out or tired of serving. She will give brand-new people in your church an opportunity to begin relationships and make friends.

You can accept it or resist it, but it's true, nonetheless. You grow at the edges.

—Tim

Show Them
the Ropes

"Since a dull ax requires great strength, sharpen the blade. That's the
value of wisdom; it helps you succeed"
(ECCLESIASTES 10:10, NLT).

If your church's ministry philosophy is similar to Granger's, you're
very interested in the experiences of your guests or visitors when
they walk through your doors for the first time. Since we're competing
with the culture and the marketplace rather than with other churches,
we've found it necessary to review how we prepare our ministry teams
for the weekend services. We're trying to deliver an experience that
rivals or exceeds what people are accustomed to getting when they
visit the theater or the mall, for example. We're trying to remove any
barriers that would prevent someone from hearing about Jesus in our
services.

In order to pull that off, we can't just expect volunteers to deliver
quality interactions and services without some intentional team
building. We try to recruit volunteers who are wired for these roles
and are trained before they serve. When people walk through our
doors for the first time, we want them to meet lots of smiling people,
encounter volunteers who are prepared to answer the questions newcomers ask, and find assistance whenever it's needed. Just like a business that places a high value on customer service, we've learned it's
important to train our ministry teams so that we can guarantee a
positive experience for our guests.

In Chapter 74, "Just-in-Time Training," Tim describes when and
how to use on-the-job training for volunteers. However, there are other
times when it's helpful to equip volunteers in advance of when they
serve. Here are some examples:

Guest Services—It's helpful to train volunteers who welcome guests before they serve for the first time. This will give you a chance to discuss with them how they should dress, greet guests, respond to questions, and serve those who need assistance. This will help ensure a great first impression for your guests.

Data Entry—This is one area that requires volunteers who are committed to excellence. Bad data entry leads to bad data, and that leads to poor communication and bad decision making. Before anyone touches your database, he or she needs to be trained.

Support Groups—It is essential that volunteers who will be helping with counseling or support groups are trained to provide effective care.

There are several ways to provide quality training in advance. Sometimes it can be handled in group orientations. Other times you'll need to do the training one-on-one. Once people are initially trained, schedule periodic reviews to help them keep their skills up-to-date. This will also provide opportunities for your leaders to recast the vision and remind the volunteers of the key core values that should shape the delivery of all your ministry services.

Your guests deserve a quality experience. Your members deserve accuracy when you're tracking their ministry connections in your database. Those who receive counseling and support deserve appropriate care. People may be volunteering their time, but your guests don't know that. If they haven't grown up in the church, their expectations don't change just because they happen to be in a church. Clearly, the hope is that we'll be able to effectively remove barriers by promoting excellence in our ministries. In order for that to happen, there will be times when you'll need to show your volunteers the ropes before they serve.

—Tony

Selling in the Church

Picture this scenario: A team of volunteers is formed to do something significant in the church. They begin meeting every week, and after a couple of months, they've formed friendships, and they all really look forward to their times together. There is a feeling of mutual care and concern. People begin to share their personal feelings and burdens, and everyone rallies when someone is down or in need.

Then one evening while at home, each member gets a call from the leader. At first, they are encouraged because he asks how they are doing and tells them that he is praying for them. But soon the conversation takes a turn, and the real purpose becomes evident. "I've recently invested in a business that is really making a difference in my life," he begins. "I'd love to talk to you about how you might invest too. You'll be amazed at how little energy it takes and how much more time you'll have to invest in church activities. I thought of you last week when you mentioned the financial pressure you and your wife are facing, and this type of opportunity might really be helpful for the two of you..."

Suddenly the entire relationship has changed. No longer is it Christian to Christian. No longer is it leader to group member. No longer is the primary interest the spiritual growth of the others. No, the team members now feel like potential clients. They wonder, "Does our leader see spiritual potential when he looks at us, or does he just see dollar signs?"

Whether you sell detergent or used cars, scrapbooks or kitchen knives, phone cards or life insurance—these types of direct-sell businesses have the potential to put a strain on the healthy relationships you've developed with your team. Once you initiate the conversation and turn your friend into a potential client, you risk losing trust. That individual may no longer trust you even when your motives are pure.

"How do I know if she really wants to help me or if she just wants to sell me more laundry detergent?" "How do I know if he's listening because he cares or if he's listening because he wants me to trust him with my investments?" Most of us are skeptical, and these questions go through our minds.

The reality is, however, that many people are self-employed and their livelihood depends on finding customers to buy their products. Many times their customers are found through word-of-mouth and networking through friends. Are we church leaders talking out of both sides of our mouths when we encourage people to build relationships at church and then forbid them to do any networking through those relationships?

This is a valid question. Here are some guidelines that you may want to consider as you address it in your setting:

- I would strongly discourage pastors, staff members, and lay leaders from selling anything *directly* to individuals in your church. Most people feel pressured by sales pitches whether they come via a phone call at dinnertime or from a friend who is "just trying to help." That is not a pressure you need as you try to help people in your church take their next spiritual steps. When you talk about Jesus, you don't want to be in a position that will cause people to question your motives. Also, an inequity of power exists between a pastor or church leader and a church member. By its nature, the relationship has the potential to make the church member feel manipulated or coerced.

- When you start a new team or group, lay some ground rules. Communicate your mission clearly, and talk about what your mission is *not*. Tell members there will be a time when everyone may talk about what they do professionally, but one-on-one selling won't be a part of your group's culture.

- Let them know that you will never approach them about your product unless they initiate the conversation. After all the members of the group have been given the opportunity to talk about what they do for a living, it's OK to say, "I'm a representative of _____, and we sell _____. If I can ever be of service to you, please let me know." This will immediately set people at ease.

Introducing your friends to vacuum cleaners, nutritional supplements, or lipstick while getting a commission and beating your monthly sales quota is not a bad thing. However, the church's mission is to introduce our friends to a life-changing relationship with Jesus that helps them find the purpose for which they were created. That is the priority. And that beats detergent any day of the week.

—Tim

68

Discover the Path to "Yes"

"Jesus called out to them, 'Come, be my disciples, and I will show
you how to fish for people!' "
(MATTHEW 4:19, NLT).

No matter what your ministry area is, your chances of having
someone commit to serving as a volunteer in a particular
capacity will increase if you follow the model that Jesus demonstrated
for us. Let's take a look at how Jesus invited Peter and Andrew to join
his ministry team.

"Come..." First, you'll notice that Jesus communicated with them
in person. He could have sent someone else. He could have written
them a letter. Instead, he met them in person, on their turf. In ministry
today, it's a lot easier to pick up the phone, send an e-mail message, or
send someone else to make the request. Jesus demonstrated that ministry begins with relationships. He built his team face to face. By taking
the time to meet Peter and Andrew in person, Jesus was indirectly communicating, "What I'm about to ask you to do is significant, and I've
determined you're the ones I want to step up. In fact, it's so important
that I've come to ask you in person."

Additionally, Jesus was clear about his purpose. He asked them to
"come." He didn't say, "You might want to consider this." He didn't say,
"When things slow down in your lives, I have an opportunity for you."
Jesus didn't give Peter and Andrew all the reasons they should say no.
Instead, he came right out and asked for a commitment. He knew he
had the right people for the role, so he confidently invited them to step
up to the call.

Let me add one more key point here. Often the most qualified people for a specific role are already busy doing something else. It may be

work related. It may be another social cause. If they're quality people with a high capacity to serve or lead, it's very likely that someone else has already asked them to do something. It could be, however, that they've elected to choose another place to invest their time because they've never heard about the opportunities to serve Jesus in ministry. You may be the person that God uses to help communicate a new call to them. Let *them* choose their priorities. Let *them* choose how to invest their time. Don't make the decision for them.

"Be my disciples…" Next, Jesus defined the role. In ministry, that includes letting people know specifically what you want them to do. Review the description outlining the responsibilities of the ministry role. Explain why you think the person has the right mix of gifts, personality, and experiences to succeed (see Chapter 53, "It *Is* My Job"). Additionally, this is a good time to talk about the expected time commitment.

"I will show you…" Jesus also defined the ongoing relationship. He promised to show them the ropes. In doing so, he was letting Peter and Andrew know that he would train and mentor them. Jesus was indicating, "I'm on this journey with you, and we're going to carry out this mission together." Volunteers in our ministries want to know how they'll be connected to others. They'll be asking themselves, "Who's going to train me? To whom can I go with questions? Who's going to cheer for me and pray for me?"

"…to fish for people." Finally, Jesus defined the mission. This is the most important step in getting to "yes." Do you wonder why Rick Warren's book *The Purpose-Driven Life* has been a best seller? People are looking for *purpose* in their lives. They want their lives to count. They want to know they're making a positive difference in the lives of others. With that in mind, don't shrink from sharing the vision. Tell them how the ministry role will affect them, the team, and the kingdom.

By following Jesus' example, you will find more people leaving their nets to answer the call.

—Tony

69

Someone Must Champion Ministry Connections

Unless it's someone's job, it's no one's job."

I learned that principle many years ago when I traveled the country with Life Action Ministries (www.lifeaction.org). For ten months each year, I joined twenty college-age students and traveled from church to church in an effort to breathe life back into the believers. We used buses or vans for transportation and carried all of our earthly possessions and equipment in semitrailers. The trucks were supremely organized, and there was "a place for everything, with everything in its place" (another one of our favorite phrases).

When we arrived at a church, we would unload thousands of pounds of audio and visual equipment, volumes of notebooks and handouts, entire offices that we would then set up in remote classrooms in the church, and all the personal belongings of the team members. Three weeks later, when it was time to load everything back into the truck, it took some major organization and focus to make sure that nothing was left behind.

That's when I learned the truth of the maxim "Unless it's someone's job, it's no one's job." Only if a piece of equipment was specifically assigned to someone did it have a chance of getting back on the truck. So, like a multi-layered corporation, we divided our team according to responsibilities and tasks. Like a well-oiled machine, we loaded everything into the truck and headed off for the next city.

> Unless someone is responsible, things often are left undone.

This is true in your family and in your business as well, isn't it? Unless someone is responsible, things often are left undone. Your kids don't clear the table and clean their rooms without some clear assignments, right? At the office, you may have a great meeting with lots of tremendous ideas, but unless someone is assigned to follow up or carry the ball, you've just wasted everyone's time.

It's crucial that someone in every ministry at your church is thinking about empowering volunteers. If it's not someone's job to help train volunteers, then it won't get done. If it's not someone's job to help with volunteer orientation, then it won't get done. If it's not someone's job to make sure the volunteers in your ministry are being celebrated, trained, and cared for, these things won't get done.

At the macro-level of your church, you need a champion for connecting people in ministry. You can say, "Connecting people in ministry is the job of every staff member." That's fine, and it sounds good, but who is responsible for this at the churchwide level? Who is figuring out how to help your people identify their spiritual gifts? Who is coming alongside ministry leaders and helping them with their training processes? Who is monitoring the church's temperature to see if you are gaining or losing leaders and volunteers?

At Granger, that person is Mark Waltz. He is our pastor of connections, and he is our champion for ministry connections. At your church it may be a volunteer, or it may be the senior pastor. It could be your music or youth pastor who has the added role of "ministry connection champion." It doesn't really matter who it is, as long as that person is passionate about seeing people plugged in to ministry.

On the road, not having clear assignments meant that a computer could be left in Dothan, Alabama, or a microphone in Paducah, Kentucky. In the church, the stakes are a lot higher. It means lives without purpose, burned-out volunteers, and impotent ministry. And those stakes are way too high.

—Tim

Mentor Your Ministry Mates

"Paul and Silas went first to Derbe and then on to Lystra.
There they met Timothy, a young disciple"
(ACTS 16:1a, NLT).

Who are the Timothys in your life? Are you showing the ropes to someone? Maybe we should be asking the bigger question: Where can we find a mentor like Paul? Can you imagine what that must have been like?

One of the greatest pictures in Scripture of a mentoring relationship is that between Paul and Timothy. Through their relationship, we can learn some great lessons about how to mentor volunteer leaders. Let's look at a handful of examples of how Paul handled this responsibility:

Paul was selective in choosing whom to mentor. That's what caused him and Barnabas to go their separate ways. Barnabas wanted to take John Mark, but Paul saw a couple of character flaws in John Mark that made him reluctant to invest time in that relationship (see Acts15:36-41). As leaders with a limited amount of time, we also must be selective about whom we ask to join our team.

Paul asked Timothy to go along on the journey. It wasn't just classroom training. Paul didn't recommend a couple of good leadership books and then toss Timothy into ministry. Instead, Paul invited Timothy to join him on the journey (see Acts 16:3). This offered Timothy the opportunity to watch Paul in action and experience hands-on training that prepared Timothy well beyond what he may have heard through Paul's teaching alone.

Paul prayed for Timothy. "Timothy, I thank God for you…Night and day I constantly remember you in my prayers" (2 Timothy 1:3, NLT).

What an encouragement it must have been for Timothy to know that his mentor was calling on God to bless his ministry. You pray for those who are reached by your ministry. You pray for your own specific ministry goals. When was the last time you prayed for the ministry impact of those who are serving on your team? When is the last time you told those people you were praying for them?

Paul asked others to set Timothy up for success. In 1 Corinthians 16:10, Paul demonstrates the importance of preparing the way for young leaders. He told the Corinthian believers, "If Timothy comes, see to it that he has nothing to fear while he is with you, for he is carrying on the work of the Lord, just as I am." Paul was encouraging others to honor and respect this new leader.

Paul also spoke highly of Timothy. For example, in 1 Corinthians 4:17 Paul described Timothy as "my son whom I love, who is faithful in the Lord." That type of praise not only increased Timothy's confidence as a leader, but it also positioned him well with those to whom he would minister. The words we use about others on a team carry great weight. We must be careful to choose words that will build up those whom God has entrusted to our leadership and care.

> We must be careful to choose words that will build up those whom God has entrusted to our leadership and care.

With that kind of mentorship, is it any wonder that Timothy found success in ministry? Now I ask the question again. Who are the Timothys in your life? Now is the time to identify whom you will build up to expand the cause of Christ. Paul demonstrated the importance of developing this type of relationship, and it's our responsibility as leaders to continue finding young Timothys to increase our ministry impact. We can't do it on our own. We must find others who will join us on the journey.

—Tony

71

Hire Leaders, Not Doers

When we hired Kem, she had spent the previous ten years in the marketplace working in the communications field. Kem doesn't know how to program in HTML, but we hired her part time to oversee our Web strategy. On the surface, it might seem like a horrible ministry fit. She doesn't know how to do Web programming or development, but we've hired her to be in charge of our Web sites.

Karen can't sing. She can't play an instrument. She can't dance or create media or act. Even with that in mind, we hired Karen to lead the entire creative arts ministry at Granger. She oversees about a dozen staff members and a couple of hundred volunteers. These are the teams that provide the music, drama, videos, and all the other artistic elements in our weekend services. Karen's previous experience? She was a school-teacher. Doesn't seem to make sense, does it?

Both of these hiring decisions are examples of hiring leaders rather than doers. Though Kem can't program a Web site, she is remarkably gifted in the areas of team development and project management. She knows how to get the right resources in the right place at the right time. Likewise, Karen has a rare gift that enables her to bring the best out of a group of artists. I've heard a couple of people compare attempts to lead artists to trying to herd cats. It can be challenging, but the results can be very rewarding. Karen has the wonderful ability to help artists express themselves and worship God while sticking to schedules and delivering on commitments.

> A talented doer often has difficulty building and leading teams.

In both of these areas and others, the tendency is to go out and find the most talented doer available and make that person the leader. For example, in the area of worship, you may be looking for someone who

169

has a great voice and can play guitar, but you don't consider whether he or she has any leadership gifts. The trouble is that a talented doer often has difficulty building and leading teams. That will become a problem as your ministry grows and you need more volunteers to reach more people. A better formula is to find a leader with passions for the specific ministry area who can build teams and lead them effectively. That's what we've done with Kem and Karen. Their success isn't measured by their individual performance; it's measured by the performance of their staff and volunteer teams.

The key here is to hire leaders whenever possible, no matter what the position is. Whether the opening is in the area of worship, care, small groups, or children, hire someone with leadership abilities. Even for our clerical staff and administrative assistant positions, we're trying to hire people who have some leadership gifts. They need these gifts to develop volunteer teams that can assist in all areas of our ministry.

When you have leaders in each ministry area, there's no limit to the growth your ministry can experience. Hire leaders, and the best will follow.

—Tony

72

Create a System for Encouragement

"Let's see how inventive we can be in encouraging love and helping out"
(HEBREWS 10:24, THE MESSAGE).

I have a friend who just oozes encouragement. Nearly every time he opens his mouth, he is encouraging someone. I've heard him saying nice things to his wife, his kids, his employees, his brother and sister, and his friends. He doesn't order food at a restaurant without making the waitress feel better about her day. He doesn't buy gas or withdraw money from a bank without making someone feel good. He jots notes of encouragement nearly every week to someone he noticed. Sometimes I think if he were shot in the back he would compliment the gunman on his accuracy.

I think I was on a different assembly line! When my friend was getting the "encourage one another all the time" wiring, I was not. For me, encouragement takes discipline. It takes thought and planning. It takes a system.

Some people think encouragement counts only if it's spontaneous. We think, "If I have to be reminded, then I may as well not say anything because I didn't really mean it." After all, if you really meant it you would have thought of it without being reminded, right?

> We build systems and discipline in order to become who we want to be.

Not necessarily. I mean, how far do you take that thinking? Do you think if you have to be reminded to take your blood pressure pill, then you probably shouldn't take it at all? Do you think if you have to have an external reminder (like a good friend or a Bible verse) to keep you from having an affair, then you probably should go ahead and do it anyway since deep in your heart you really want to? Do you think that if you must have a system in order to exercise or eat right or read the Bible, then you should just ignore all those things because your heart isn't really in it?

Of course not. We build systems and discipline in order to become who we want to be. We want to have integrity in our marriages, so we build external accountability and boundaries so we won't fall. We want to be healthy, so we develop systems for exercise and proper eating.

If you want to be an encourager, then build systems and habits into your life to help you become one. Here are some different ideas you could try:

Write three postcards a week. On Sunday afternoon when the services have concluded, don't go home until you have written some postcards to volunteers who you noticed were making a difference with their lives.

Block thirty minutes a week for encouragement. It's a good habit to write an "encouragement appointment" on your calendar every week. Take half an hour to think about the people you need to encourage, and then encourage them.

Go for a walk. At Granger, our offices are spread throughout the entire building. I can go for a week or more without seeing certain staff members. Occasionally, I'll just go for a walk without an agenda. Well, I guess I do have an agenda: I want to see and encourage as many staff members as I can. Sometimes I do this on Sunday morning, walking through the children's ministry rooms to see and encourage volunteers. It's amazing what a few well-placed, meaningful words can do for someone.

Write or e-mail. Know your personality, and use written encouragement if it works better for you. It does for me. People don't spend time with me and say, "Wow, he sure was warm and pleasant." I never hear, "I felt as if I'd known him my whole life." Sometimes it's a challenge for me to verbalize my feelings about a person. I'm working on that, but I've found that my encouragement is a lot more significant if I put it in writing. People realize that I'm not saying these things just to keep the conversation going, but because I was thinking about them when they weren't around. That can be very meaningful, and they'll remember it for a long time.

So if you're like me at all, take the time right now to create a system that will help you remember to encourage those around you. If, on the other hand, you're an "encouragement oozer" like my friend, then let me encourage you to keep encouraging others so we all can become better encouragers.

—Tim

73

It's Not a Life Sentence

Here's something we've learned to make it easier for people to say yes to serving in ministry. Let them know upfront that there's an end date to their commitment. Make it six months or a school year, but make sure there's some sort of "opt out" date. People will be more likely to commit to a new ministry if they know it's something they can try out, and then they may move on if it's not a good fit.

The advantage of this is that it removes the guilt. The last thing you want is for people to serve in a ministry because they feel guilty about quitting. Some of us have experienced the nightmare of offering to fill in for someone one Sunday morning, and then, three years later, we're still waiting for that person to return. You need people who are fully committed to the mission and passionate about their specific roles. It's not helpful when people are just going through the motions because they think they *have* to do it.

This gives people the freedom to try out several ministries and find the ones that best fit them. It's not unusual for people to discover new spiritual gifts because they had a chance to test-drive several ministries. This is a huge benefit to the church because more people end up serving in roles in which they soar, and that increases the impact of the entire church.

At the end of each cycle of ministry, recast the vision and allow your team members to recommit to the next run. This will give some people the chance to reaffirm their commitments. Others will be relieved to know that they can try something else. This process helps you build a more cohesive team. It increases trust and unity. All the members of the team know that the people they're serving beside are pulling in the same direction because they're not being pressured to stay. They're all there because they actually look forward to serving.

Taking these steps shifts the focus from a "help wanted" mentality, in which you're looking for "warm bodies" to fill roles, to a culture in which you're helping people get plugged into ministries that fulfill their life purpose.

Don't box people in to specific ministries. Give them the freedom to try out new opportunities and to do so without guilt.

—Tony

74

Just-in-Time Training

Let's pretend that there are one hundred things to know in order to become a leader at your church. The extremes on the scale might look something like this:

0 = I know nothing. I don't know this church; I don't know how to lead; I couldn't even lead someone to the bathroom.

100 = I know almost everything there is to know about leading a team at this church, and I'm always learning more. I'm not only effective at leading a group of volunteers, but I'm also good at training others to become effective leaders.

Bearing this scale in mind, consider several types of training philosophies in different churches:

The "What Scale?" Philosophy—At these churches, there are no systems for support, encouragement, or measurement. Anyone can lead if he or she is smart enough to figure out who to talk to. People can lead anyone they want because there aren't any rules to break or lines to cross. There is no structure. This will work for a while in a small church, but eventually it will begin to frustrate high-capacity volunteers or leaders.

The "100 Club" Philosophy—These churches have extensive training systems in place. If you want to be a leader, you have to be at the "100 level," and it may take months or even years to jump through all the hoops to get there. There will be books to read, classes and seminars to attend, and tests to take. You'll be involved in "leader-in-training" mentoring programs, and you may even have to undergo the "laying on of hands by the elders" before you are recognized as a leader.

In my opinion, the 100 Club philosophy will work in a small to medium-sized church that has either plateaued or is growing very slowly. This philosophy, in and of itself, will be a "lid" preventing the church from growing at a healthy pace. With an extensive leadership training process like this, the church will be unable to turn out leaders fast enough to sustain growth. The defenders of this system might say that this will be a healthier church in the long term. But is a "healthy" church that is not effectively reaching more and more of its community really all that healthy?

The "See Who's Following" Philosophy—The model we've chosen at Granger is to look behind the leader to see who's following. You aren't a leader because we say you are. You are a leader because people are following you. You aren't a leader because a church has put you in a position and given you a title. You are a leader because you are leading people (profound, huh?).

John Maxwell talks about this in slightly different terms in his book *The 21 Irrefutable Laws of Leadership*. He says, "People don't follow others by accident. They follow individuals whose leadership they respect. Someone who is an 8 in leadership...doesn't go out and look for a 6 to follow—he naturally follows a 9 or 10. The less skilled follow the more highly skilled and gifted."[1]

At Granger we employ "just-in-time" training in many areas of our ministry. We tell you enough upfront to orient you to the ministry, and then we let you jump in and start serving. For example, in our All Stars Children's Ministry, orientation is a forty-five-minute overview session. After that you start serving, and we tell you everything else as you need to know it...just in time.

You try to teach your sixteen-year-old son how to change a diaper, and he couldn't care less. He'll blow you off. Why? It's irrelevant to his life. The information goes in one ear and out the other. You talk to him six years later when he has a newborn at home and his wife is on her first shopping trip alone—he's all ears. He'll be listening, taking notes, drawing diagrams in his PDA, and recording voice notes in his digital recorder. That's called just-in-time training. It's on a need-to-know basis, and he definitely needs to know!

Of course you'll have to require certain levels of skill or spiritual maturity for people in some positions (see Chapter 44, "Easy Access Is Crucial"), but don't fool yourself into thinking that every position in your church requires the spiritual maturity of Mother Teresa.

—Tim

ENDNOTE

1. John C. Maxwell, *The 21 Irrefutable Laws of Leadership* (Nashville, TN: Thomas Nelson, Inc., 1998), 70-71.

75

Embrace the Tough Conversations

Here's one thing I've noticed about growing churches. As the number of people who gather for a weekend service increases, the expectations for music quality also grow. The same holds true for teaching. As the number of people attending a class or listening to a message increases, the expectations for the teaching quality also increase. In fact, this principle is true throughout your church's ministry. As numbers increase, so will expectations. Read more about this in Chapter 28, "Quality Attracts Quality."

The tough part about this is that sometimes the skills and abilities of volunteers don't keep pace with the growth of the church. That means, for example, that an actor on the drama team who performed well when two hundred people were attending services may not be the best fit for two thousand people. The person hasn't changed; the church has. This can lead to difficulties for leaders because sometimes volunteers don't recognize this on their own, and it is up to their leaders to help them understand that their abilities are no longer a good match for their current roles.

> Sometimes the skills and abilities of volunteers don't keep pace with the growth of the church.

As difficult as these conversations may be, it's important that you have them. You can't let people who are poor fits for ministry roles continue to serve in those roles. It's not good for the church because poor quality, particularly in ministries visible to newcomers, can turn people away from your church. If you can't meet or exceed the expectations of your guests who don't yet know Christ, they won't return. When that happens, you're essentially saying that the church is here to serve the volunteers.

These conversations are also important for the people who are no longer good fits for their ministry roles. For one thing, you're saving them the embarrassment of trying to serve in roles for which they're obviously not qualified. As Christ-followers, we're called to encourage one another, to build one another up. We're not supposed to let people serve in roles that embarrass them or the cause of Christ.

> Every moment that we let people continue to serve in poorly fitting roles takes them away from ministries in which they could soar.

Additionally, every moment that we let people continue to serve in poorly fitting roles takes them away from ministries in which they could soar. We're denying them the opportunity to serve as God has best gifted them.

Here are some suggestions to help both you and the volunteer walk away from these tough conversations encouraged and positioned to have the greatest impact for the kingdom.

Establish trust. If you work to maintain authentic relationships characterized by open, honest communication, these types of conversations will be normal rather than exceptional.

Ask questions. Begin by letting the volunteer tell his or her story. What is still challenging about the role? What is frustrating? You could be surprised to find that the volunteer already feels somewhat disconnected from his or her current role.

Be honest. Deep down, people want to know how they can improve—and how they are hitting the ball out of the park. If people respect your leadership, they will also respect your honest assessment of their strengths and weaknesses.

Offer training suggestions. Sometimes people may have to step out of active serving roles until their skills have improved. Suggest lessons. Point out training seminars. Offer coaching opportunities if they're available. Many of the most accomplished baseball players, for example, had to spend some time in the minor leagues, fine-tuning their skills until they were ready for the big leagues.

Identify new roles. A different role may be available in the same ministry. This would allow a person to continue serving in the area about which he or she is passionate, but in a better-fitting position.

Don't delay. Silence communicates the message "You're still a good fit," and it makes the ultimate conversation much more difficult.

If you have had an open and honest relationship, it shouldn't come as a surprise to people when you ask them to stop serving in specific roles.

End with encouragement. Finish the conversation by pointing out these individuals' strengths. Remind them that you want the best for them and that you're prepared to help them succeed in ministry.

A good leader constantly evaluates prospective and existing volunteers to make sure they are serving in the best places for themselves and the ministry. That's one of the great opportunities of a growing ministry. As the church grows, the number of unique ministry roles also grows, which means that someone whose gifts and abilities no longer match the needs of one role will likely have several other ministry options from which to choose.

Encourage your volunteers by helping them find the ministry roles that will allow them to soar. Don't let people continue to serve where they can't be all God intended them to be. It's not good for the church, and it's certainly not good for the people who want to be where Jesus has called them to serve.

—Tony

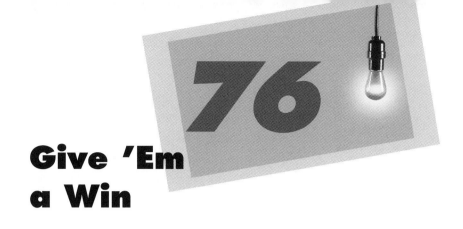

Give 'Em a Win

Recently my six-year-old, Hunter, was working on his Christmas list. He came to two items that cost $11.99 each, and it took him about thirty seconds to add them together in his head (without using his fingers). I've met many adults who couldn't do that kind of math as quickly with a calculator!

When Hunter began learning math, he didn't start with calculus. You don't throw a trigonometry question at a six-year-old. Complex fractions or long division problems are not typically where you start. Why? You want to give the child an early win. You want him to have some successes under his belt before you throw something more challenging at him. If a child is constantly bombarded with problems that are too difficult, he will eventually become discouraged and stop trying.

The same holds true throughout life, especially with volunteers. A man can feel very secure and confident in his profession or in his role as a husband and father, but he could come to church as a volunteer and feel very much like a fish out of water. You need to look for ways to give "early wins" to your volunteers—and to celebrate those wins.

Let's say you're in charge of the nursery at your church. Five other volunteers have been helping you for years, but you really need more. So the pastor does a big "make a difference with your life" type of service, and Bob and Susan sign up to be on your team.

Your team is happy for the help. However, they don't know Bob and Susan well enough yet to trust them. Conversely, Bob and Susan don't know your team. They aren't convinced they'll even like your team, and they are nervous about their new roles.

They don't know what they're supposed to do, and everything feels awkward. They know your team has been together for years, so they feel a bit like they're at someone else's family reunion.

> You want to reduce the tension and awkwardness and give them confidence right away.

It's your job to give them a win as fast as you possibly can! You want to reduce the tension and awkwardness and give them confidence right away. Here are two ideas:

Listen carefully to their words. If Susan has an idea, even if it's not a new idea, let the whole group know what a great idea Susan had. It will quickly give her (and the team) a sense that she is adding value. And it will give Susan the confidence to be an active participant on the team.

Make sure you place people in roles they like. One of the worst things you can do to volunteers is to place them in positions that meet *your* need rather than those that fit *their* passions and gifts. After a few weeks, ask Bob and Susan how they feel, what they enjoy, and what they suggest.

Whatever your strategy may be, keep in mind the need to create an early win for every new volunteer. Whether it's a six-year-old facing a math problem or a forty-six-year-old stepping into a role in the church nursery, we all need to be affirmed so we can each take our next step with confidence.

—Tim

77

Let People
Tell Their Stories

"I am praying not only for these disciples but also for all who will
ever believe in me because of their testimony"
(JOHN 17:20, NLT).

In a planned interruption of the pastor's message, Tammy recently
shared her story about coming to Granger Community Church
with her husband and their twin girls. At the time they started attending weekend services, she was deeply involved in her career. She had
accepted a management position with her employer, which is what
necessitated the transfer that had brought her to Granger.

Tammy was asked to share her story during all five of the weekend's
services. The service series was designed to help people discover how
God has created each of us uniquely and for a purpose. It's the stuff that
we preach about often, but sometimes people hear it more clearly when
it comes from a peer rather than a professional minister.

Tammy explained how God had prompted her to refocus her time
and energy on her family. As a result, she left her job to be at home full
time with her girls. She wasn't suggesting that this is the right decision
for everyone, but it was clearly the right decision for her. Within several days of making the transition, she was diagnosed with breast cancer. She also learned that she was a few weeks pregnant.

Tammy explained that, during this crisis, she and her husband were
connected with a small group and found places to serve even while she
was facing surgeries and chemotherapy. Since that time, she has recovered from the treatments, is in perfect health, and has a new baby girl,
Mia Grace. Tammy explained how God has used both her former career
and her battle with cancer to help others in her ministry at Granger.

These are the stories that stir our emotions, but they also cause us to reflect on our unique design and life purpose. By hearing Tammy describe how important it was for her to have the support of small-group and ministry-team relationships during her treatments and pregnancy, others felt challenged to have those same types of relational opportunities. When they heard how Tammy used the leadership skills God gave her to find significance in her ministry role, others were motivated to take steps into ministry.

People can tell their stories in many ways. We've had people give live testimonials during the message. Sometimes we ask people to read their testimonies, and other times we ask one of the teaching pastors to interview them. We've also used video to capture testimonies. The advantage of the video method is that you can capture images of the person serving or sharing life with others in a way that's not possible when the person is speaking from the platform. People love to hear how God has transformed lives. It's all about sharing how people have experienced life change.

> People love to hear how God has transformed lives.

Let people tell their stories. There's no better way to describe how God has used your ministry to change lives, and there's no better way to show people how stepping into ministry could affect themselves and others.

—Tony

78

Hire Your Volunteers

There is a very important principle that we wrote about in our first book, *Simply Strategic Stuff*. It is so critical that we believe we should reiterate it: When you are ready to hire someone, always look within your church at the current volunteers before you ever look outside your church.

This is not how most churches hire. Most believe that they need someone from outside to take them to "the next level." Or they need the expertise and skills of the guy coming from seminary. Or they need someone to challenge the status quo and help them figure out new and different ways to do ministry. Or they need someone who has been where they want to go.

All of this may be true, but there are several things that you must also factor into the decision. These are aspects of the decision that most churches forget to consider:

You can't underestimate your DNA. There are things that make your church unique. Yes, these include your written mission, vision, and values statements, but they also include personality, leadership style, culture, and many other qualities that will never be captured on paper. These are the things you can't always ask your out-of-town candidate to agree to. They are often the intangibles, and the incompatibility of an "outsider" may not appear for months or years.

You can't underestimate chemistry. This may be one of the most overlooked areas in hiring. You have to like your team. You have to enjoy the people you work with. If someone is coming to oversee your music ministry, you must be reasonably certain that the volunteers in that area will like the "new guy" and want to work with him. If you hire someone from within your church, you already know about his or her relationships with the people in the church. You already know whether the person is respected and influential.

You can't underestimate authenticity. You can ask all the questions you want in an interview, you can do a dozen different tests, and you can call a hundred references, but you still don't get close to the truth about candidates until you live with them and watch them in everyday life. You need to see how they react when they're squeezed and when they're attacked. You need to watch them when everything falls apart at the last minute or when their budgets get slashed to almost nothing. When you hire a faithful and proven volunteer, you significantly reduce your chances of being surprised.

At Granger, forty-eight of our fifty-five staff members have been hired from among our volunteers. Among our eleven pastors, six were hired from within the church. In our seventeen-year history, 95 percent of our inside hires have been successful. That is, they are still on staff, or they left without difficulty. On the other hand, only 50 percent of our outside hires have been successful.

It is a principle that we embrace wholeheartedly, and we believe it is one of the reasons that we have low staff turnover. When you have low turnover, you can focus more time on the core of your ministry and less on staff replacement issues.

And it is a principle we have practiced. Corey was a radio DJ at the top-rated station in town, and we hired him to lead our high school ministry (it tripled in size in the first twelve months of Corey's leadership). Melanie ran a restaurant and is now our facilities manager. Blair was a day trader and now leads our small-group ministries. Karen was a middle school teacher, and is now our creative arts pastor. All of them, including Tony and I, were volunteers at Granger before we ever joined the staff.

You have people in your church who (1) love God, (2) understand your church's vision, (3) are highly capable, (4) have proven themselves to be leaders at your church and in their jobs, (5) love you, (6) are enjoyable to be around, (7) have skills you need, and (8) are currently serving faithfully.

My recommendation: *Hire them as soon as you can.*

—Tim

Preparation Is as Important as the Event

As a leader, one of your most important functions is coaching behind the scenes before big events. Whether your team is preparing for a weekend service, an outreach effort, or the launch of a new ministry, the preparation usually takes many more hours and much more effort than the event itself. A good coach, however, can keep the team focused on the end results. Additionally, a lot of ministry can occur before the event takes place. Your volunteers will have opportunities to share their lives with you as you prepare, which will allow you to encourage one another in several areas, including your faith journeys.

We were recently preparing for a big event at Granger. We are a satellite location for the Leadership Summit that Bill Hybels offers every August (www.willowcreek.com). For several months leading up to the summit, we had at least a dozen different teams getting ready for the three-day event and the pre-conference workshops. As you can imagine, there was quite a bit to accomplish in the final days leading up to the summit. Many staff members and volunteers worked long days to ensure a positive experience for our guests. Here's an excerpt from a message I sent to our team as we were nearing the home stretch:

After months and months of planning, the big event is finally here! We're hosting almost 150 leaders on Wednesday for our WiredChurches.com workshops. The next day we have 500 church leaders and GCCers here for the Leadership Summit Thursday through Saturday. I can't wait to see how God uses these events to ramp up leaders for their next run of ministry. People will be inspired. Churches will be changed. And many more people will meet Jesus in the future because of what happens at Granger over these next several days. That's way too cool to even comprehend.

But, as you all know, there's more to the event than the event. There are all the preliminary communications, tasks, and prayers that help launch a conference or a service or a new ministry program with success. And don't you feel it? There's a buzz in the building today, and it's going to grow louder until Bill Hybels steps up to the podium on Thursday morning. The facilities team is cranking. Volunteers are receiving training. Administrative staff are preparing materials. The receptionist is answering lots of calls. I love weeks like this! Ministry is happening!

So in the midst of the long hours and the last-minute details, don't forget to step back and praise God for all he's doing in our midst. Only a few churches have been selected to participate in the Leadership Summit. Well over 30,000 church leaders will be participating on Willow's campus and at the various satellite locations. Revival is taking place in the church across America, and we get to be on the front lines. Enjoy the event. But also enjoy the preparation.

I've heard Mark Beeson, our senior pastor, remind us that preparation communicates value and importance. When you spend time vacuuming and cooking before guests visit your house, it tells them when they arrive, "We were expecting you, and we're glad you came." The same holds true for those who participate in ministry events at your church. Your level and quality of preparation will speak volumes to your guests.

> Preparation communicates value and importance.

Additionally, preparation is important to those who are serving. It's an opportunity to remind people of your vision. It's also an opportunity to help people take their next steps toward Christ. During the preparation, people aren't just completing tasks; they're growing through the process.

If people begin to lose sight of the reason for all the time and energy spent preparing for the next event, view the situation as a teaching moment. Help your staff and volunteers stay focused on the importance of preparing well.

—Tony

Dare to Debrief

(You may have flipped through the table of contents and turned
quickly to this chapter, hoping to find some ammunition to use on
your pastor to convince him or her to preach shorter messages.
Sorry, wrong chapter. That one is called "Dare to *Be* Brief,"
which we'll be sure to include in a future book.)

Asking someone to debrief something that you have worked on
is painful! Try spending all week writing a sermon, and then
after you deliver it on Sunday, ask a dozen people to honestly analyze
what worked, what didn't, and where they felt their eyes getting heavy.
That can be tough information to swallow.

We don't debrief for several reasons. First, it takes time. And who
has extra time? We are all up to our eyeballs in meetings and responsibilities, and it's tough to take extra time for something that seems
optional. Second, sometimes we just don't care. "I don't need someone
to tell me it wasn't perfect." Third, we may not want to know. We don't
want to know what others think should be done differently and be held
accountable to those expectations next time. Finally, we don't want to
face the tension of a tough conversation when we disagree with the
solution someone has offered.

Even so, taking the time to ask others to help you evaluate the
effectiveness of an event, service, or ministry season has so many
advantages! And it can be done in creative ways in every ministry of
your church. Here are some ideas:

- With ongoing ministries (such as working with children),
  take time to annually evaluate the overall ministry with your
  top volunteer leaders. Ask them to do the same thing with

the volunteers in their departments. In what ways are you hitting the ball out of the park? Where do you need to improve?

- When teams work on events that have a definite ending date, get together a few weeks later for a celebration party. During that party, take time to debrief. What worked? What didn't? What should you change? What should you keep? What was the experience like for you? How could you organize it better next time? How was your communication?
- Establish a system for talking to new volunteers after three, six, and twelve months. Use this opportunity to make sure they are right in the middle of what they love to do. And find out if there is anything that can be organized or communicated that will provide better care for the leaders. Can you imagine how you would increase your retention rate through this type of process?
- Establish exit interviews for all the volunteers who leave your ministry. Were they cared for? Were their expectations met? Were their gifts utilized? Did they have any disappointments?

Yes, these types of conversations and meetings take time. They require intentionality. They take focus and patience and strong leadership. But they create a win-win situation all the way around.

- **The volunteers win because they are heard.** They believe that their opinions are valued. Even if they've had a bad experience, they don't feel as bad about it now because you've asked their opinions on how to make it better for others.
- **The event or project or ministry wins.** We get ideas that are really good, and we don't make the same mistakes again.
- **You win.** Those who helped you will be surprised that you're asking for their input, and if you are sincere and open, you will gain more of their respect and trust.

So face the pain. Take the time. Plan the meeting. Debrief.

One extra piece of advice: If you want your debriefs to be brief, then do a brief debrief of your debriefs. Just a thought.

—Tim

81

Let Ministry Teams Share Their Dreams

I love gathering around the kitchen table to share a meal. It's the one time during the day when my family is together and we can focus on one another. We share what's happening in our lives—our ups and downs—and talk about our dreams for the future. It's the one chance that we really have to give the entire family our undivided attention.

You also need to create opportunities for your ministry teams to share at the "kitchen table." Develop ways for staff and lay leaders and their teams to discuss events in their ministry areas with the other teams they serve beside. Allow these teams to talk about their visions for the future and what will be needed for those visions to become reality. Finally, try to create an environment in which it's natural for teams to share insights that wouldn't normally be communicated in front of the entire church.

At Granger we've used many methods to increase interaction between teams. Here are a couple of examples:

All-Staff Meetings—A portion of each weekly all-staff meeting includes a "ministry focus" segment in which we spend ten or fifteen minutes highlighting one specific ministry area. Either a staff or lay leader makes the presentation and then answers questions from the rest of the staff.

Budget Presentations—We take time during the budget process to let ministry leaders summarize action plans and goals for the coming year. This is a great opportunity for everyone to see how difficult it is to allocate limited resources across the ministry. It helps eliminate the whining that might occur when teams don't have enough information about the other areas of ministry that also require financial support.

The type of conversation you can have at the kitchen table will look very different from the type of communication that happens in front of the entire church. Kitchen-table conversations include both successes and challenges; some won't be appropriate for everyone to hear but are necessary for those who are sharing life together as a ministry team.

These conversations are helpful for several reasons. They build momentum for your team when the other teams hear what's happening in your area of the ministry. They increase the prayer effectiveness of your team. They clarify vision as people consider all the ways God is affecting lives throughout the church. They give others the information they need to refer people to other ministry areas appropriately. Additionally, they help others identify prospective volunteers who might be a good fit for the team.

In smaller churches this may not be an issue. As the size of your church and the number of ministry teams increase, you'll need to be strategic about creating times to open up dialogue among your teams. More than anything, this will help to maintain focus and unity. Without kitchen-table conversations, teams tend to focus more on their own arenas and forget that there are several ministries working toward one unified vision.

—Tony

82

You Can't Steer a Parked Car

As a teenager I drove a 1979 Plymouth Horizon. It definitely was never featured in any muscle car magazines, but my dad said that beggars can't be choosers. It ran pretty well, but I had a tendency to live on the edge and rarely filled the gas tank until it was running on fumes. Of course, that meant that I spent some time on the side of the road with my Horizon after miscalculating the number of miles left in the gas tank.

When you're driving, even very slowly, it takes just slight pressure with a finger to turn the direction of the car. However, have you ever tried to steer a parked car? It's amazingly difficult. When you're out of gas and need to push the car to the side of the road, it can take all of your efforts, and you still may not be able to budge the steering wheel.

> Forward direction and momentum are required to make good decisions about ministry effectiveness.

This principle applies to ministry as well. Forward direction and momentum are required to make good decisions about ministry effectiveness.

As a leader, I've often talked to individuals in the church who are not serving. They attend most weeks, talk as if they love the church, and tell others about the church, but they don't serve in any capacity. When I ask them about it, I get a common response: "Oh, I'm just not sure yet about my gifts or interests. I'm still praying and waiting for God to show me the right place to use my time and abilities."

You've probably been engaged in the same type of conversations. Here's some advice you can give those individuals: Start moving, and ask God to steer you into the right ministries. Don't sit on your posterior and expect God to flash it across your television screen. Jump into ministry and do something, and then ask those who know you best if they believe you're in the right ministry. Let your ministry leader know that you're exploring how God has wired you, and make a short-term commitment. Ask God to give you direction while you're taking steps in ministry.

Recently I received a copy of an e-mail sent from Daryl, one of our volunteers, that illustrates this point very well. He serves in our LiveWire ministry (Web-based technology) and was communicating with one of our vendors. Daryl started with his story:

I began attending seven years ago, but never really became involved in ministry until this year. I sat on the bench and watched from a distance. I was intrigued and inspired by the innovative tools used to communicate the gospel to the lost within our community. But it wasn't until I actually signed on with the LiveWire ministry that I realized the dedication to excellence that exists here. I viewed churches as less than effective and assumed things would be done half as well here as they are in the marketplace. But this did not occur. In fact the vision, use of technology, and commitment to excellence at Granger have been greater than anything I had seen in the "outside world."

You can clearly see how it was volunteering that pulled him into the church. Once he began serving, it became *his* church. Now he uses words such as *we* and *our*. Read on as he extends a heartfelt challenge:

First, our technology must keep up with our growth. We must ensure that our hardware, software, and third-party services are expandable. Second, we must make sure we are keeping up with technology. As new ideas turn into new technology, we need to be sure our hardware, software, and other services can adapt appropriately or be upgraded with minimal cost and effort. And finally, our "online image" must communicate our commitment to excellence. If we go where I think we are going, there is little margin for error. We can't settle for "minimum coverage," "package B," or even "This is as good as it gets." We need to nail it!

For six years, Daryl was parked. He came to church services, but he wasn't involved. Then he was invited into ministry, and now he's communicating the vision and values of the ministry with passion!

You'll learn so much about yourself, your likes and dislikes, and your passions and interests by staying engaged and active in ministry. God will be able to steer you into the ministries in which you can have the greatest impact. If you are parked, on the other hand, you will be very hard to get moving again. And the longer you're parked, the more comfortable you'll be in your sedentary state.

—Tim

83

Find People Who Get Things Done

Bev is one of those "get it done and then some" volunteers. She is the person responsible for creating the backdrops for each new weekend series. Based on the theme of each series, Bev leads the team that designs the images and then paints the flats for each stage set. One of her other volunteer roles is media creation. It takes about forty hours to create a four-minute video, and Bev does this all from her home computer, working late into the night after her family is in bed. Many of her videos are used in our weekend services throughout the year. That's not all. She also volunteers in our children's ministry by taking photographs at various kids' activities and creating pictures that line the halls of our children's center. Bev gives countless hours to the ministry at Granger. By the way, there's probably one more thing you may want to know about Bev. She has five kids between the ages of four and twelve.

So what is it that distinguishes a volunteer like Bev from the others? Why would someone commit fully to being a wife and mother—and then give hundreds of hours to serve in a ministry...or several ministries?

It begins with matching gifts and passions. Bev is a very talented artist. She's found a place in ministry that causes her to soar, a place where she serves because she wants to serve. No one's making her do it. She fully understands that her role is to help people meet Jesus and take steps in their faith journey. She loves connecting with today's culture through various forms of the arts. She has found her calling.

Second, she's prioritized her obligations to allow time to serve. Bev isn't unlike any other gifted person. There are certainly other ways she could be spending her time. She has elected, however, to give her time and gifts to the church. The most gifted people in your ministry won't have extra time, but they'll make time if the vision is clear and compelling and someone asks them to step up to serve.

Bev is also oriented to getting the job done. Some people don't wait for someone else to lead the charge. They are dissatisfied with the status quo. They're like Nehemiah, who returned to Jerusalem to find the city's walls in disrepair and recognized that it was *his* responsibility to address the problem. He didn't go to the king to complain and try to get the king to take care of it. Nehemiah went to the king and asked if he would allow him to repair the walls. And fifty-two days later, the walls were rebuilt.

Match abilities and passions. Cast a vision to which gifted people will commit their time. Add people to your team who are action-oriented. It's part of your role as leader to identify the kinds of volunteers who help you get it done...and then some.

—Tony

84

Build Teams to Climb Mountains

Would you rather discover a cure for cancer or sweep floors at a pharmacy? Would you rather find hidden treasure in the deserts of Egypt or discover hidden trash in your backyard? Would you rather climb a mountain that's never been climbed or mow the same lawn for the ten thousandth time?

There is something in all of us that wants to do something new and exciting. We want to make a difference. We want to climb mountains or be the home run king. We want to get the gold at the Olympics or write the book that influences people's thinking for decades. It's in all of us. We want to make a difference.

That's why we should always be thinking of new ways to capture the visions and dreams of our people. How can we accomplish our mission in a way that excites people, gives them a sense that they are truly making a difference, and allows them to pioneer a meaningful cause?

To illustrate, let me ask you to consider which of the following "sales pitches" you would respond to from your church.

Option A *(spoken in an intense, bounce-off-the-wall, contagious tone)*: "This is a new day! We can't do things the way we've always done them. In order to reach more people, we're launching a new [fill in the blank]. We've never tried this before, but we think it will be successful if we get the right people involved. You may be someone who wants to get in on the ground floor, to help us build this brand-new ministry!"

Option B *(said slowly and softly in a low, monotonous voice)*: "We'll be doing the same thing this year that we did last year and the year before. In fact, it's the same thing we've been doing for more than two decades. Do you remember..." *Speaker drifts off to a seven-minute reflection of life back in the '70s...until he suddenly notices his notes.* "So we need some faithful, stable, consistent people to fill the same ol' positions. Sign up in the lobby at the same table under the same sign that we've used for years."

This illustration is a bit tongue-in-cheek, but we've all heard pitches for volunteers that sound nearly as boring as Option B. Here is some advice for building teams to climb mountains:

Let the old die. No, this isn't a plug for euthanasia. I'm talking about letting dying services or programs die. I've heard John Maxwell say about dead church programs: "If the horse is dead, for goodness' sake, dismount!" It's not the method that's sacred; it's the purpose. If the purpose for that service is still critical, then figure out a different way to accomplish it. To get new people involved, you need to repackage it and launch it anew!

Use capital campaigns to raise leaders. If you run a capital campaign in the right way, you will gain lots of new volunteers. Why? Because new people (as a whole) don't want to jump into existing programs. Those programs have been happening without them for years. They'd rather jump into something new and exciting. When you run a good stewardship campaign, you're casting a vision for how the church will be even more effective in the coming years, and you're asking for a huge portion of the church to volunteer in a number of short-term roles. This is a new and exciting prospect.

Plan big events. Strategically plan momentum-building events into your churchwide calendar every six months or so. These might include the opening of a new facility, an all-church baptism celebration, groundbreaking events, anniversary parties, or spiritual step campaigns (such as *40 Days of Purpose* from www.purposedriven.com). You can use these events to generate momentum and get new people excited about volunteering.

People want to make a difference. They want their lives to matter. Don't condemn your volunteers to lives engaged in sameness. Call the best out of them. Ask them to step up and invest their lives in a cause that will outlive them. Invite them to the adventure of a lifetime! And say it as if you mean it!

—Tim

85

Take Volunteers Along for the Ride

We just got back from INJOY's Catalyst conference (www.injoy.com). More than ninety people from our church made the trip from Indiana to Atlanta to experience leadership training and worship. Nearly seventy of those people were volunteers who paid their own way including registration fees and airfare, hotel, and meal expenses. I'm always amazed at the commitment of volunteer leaders to take time from their already busy schedules and make a financial commitment to join us for an experience like that. In the end, though, they recognize that conferences like these are going to improve their leadership skills, help them take steps in their faith journeys, and deepen their relationships with others on the ministry team.

We see the same thing happen when others travel to Granger to attend the Innovative Church conference or other workshops offered by WiredChurches.com. Some come with a team of people. Others, for a variety of reasons, experience the training on their own. Whenever possible, you should try to bring others along. When you go to a new place, immersing yourself in a new experience and learning new things, it's hard to go back and communicate what happened and how God has changed you. A lot gets lost in the translation. On the other hand, when volunteers from your team are there, you immediately have others who have already caught the vision and are ready to help champion any needed changes in direction.

This principle holds true for other opportunities as well. You can invite volunteers, particularly those with leadership roles (or potential leaders), to join you for visits to other churches. Invite them to join you for brainstorming sessions to dream about the future of the ministry. Consider bringing others along to any ministry functions or learning opportunities that you might typically participate in on your own.

You'll also want to look for special circumstances when it would be best to offer financial assistance to help volunteers join an experience. Though the vast majority of our volunteers pay their own way, we've sometimes helped volunteers attend conferences and other learning experiences. Sometimes another person sponsors a volunteer. Sometimes the church helps to cover the expenses. This is a particularly good option when you've identified a prospective leader who has demonstrated commitment to your mission and vision but may not be able to afford the event.

The next time you plan a trip to learn new ministry strategies, invite others to join you in the experience. It may require that someone coordinate the details of the trip, but it will be worth it. When you share life together away from home, you'll deepen relationships and create a synergy that helps others capture a new vision for reaching more people for Christ.

—Tony

86

Anything I Can Do, You Can Do Better

"I'm superior, you're inferior.
I'm the big attraction, you're the small.
I'm the major one, you're the minor one,
I can beat you shootin', that's not all."
—IRVING BERLIN, "ANYTHING YOU CAN DO, I CAN DO BETTER"

I sometimes wonder if these lyrics aren't the anthem of church leaders. Every time a decision must be made or a prayer must be prayed, the pastor is there. Every time a message must be preached or a person must be reached, the pastor is there. He greets, teaches, makes hospital visits, counsels misfits, and leads the singing. When there's trouble in the air, do not despair. The pastor will be there.

Now we don't come right out and say it, but aren't we really teaching our people that ministry can take place only if the pastor is around? When we step in to sprinkle our "pastor dust," aren't we saying, "I'm superior, you're inferior. Leave the ministry to the professionals"? As the church grows and the staff increases, is this value getting passed along to other paid team members as well? Are they looking at their jobs to figure out how they can equip the saints to do the ministry, or are they keeping it all to themselves?

Mark Beeson is our senior pastor. One of the things I've most respected about his leadership is his willingness to step out of ministry roles to allow the church to continue to grow. Since the very first service held in a movie theater in 1986, Mark has been giving his ministry away to others. In several instances, he's let others take over ministries that he really enjoyed and would prefer to hold on to; however, he realizes he can't do that and still accomplish the church's mission to reach more and more people for Jesus.

Take, for example, the weekend services. Mark is a gifted artist in addition to an accomplished teacher and communicator. When the church was smaller, he led worship on his twelve-string guitar. He used to prepare slide shows using his own photographs. He used to create clever cartoons to communicate visually what he was trying to teach orally. He used to select the songs and the various other elements that would support the weekly message. Mark gave up all those activities long ago. He recognized that by holding on to them, he'd be taking away opportunities for others to fulfill those ministry roles. He knew that other people would be better gifted in those areas and could focus more of their time, prayer, and energy on those functions. This, in turn, would improve the overall quality of the services. He knew that by giving up certain things, he could add the greatest value to the ministry by focusing his attention on the three or four roles God has gifted him to fulfill.

> Pastors, other paid staff members, and volunteer leaders can always find others to perform many ministry functions far better than they themselves can.

This principle holds true throughout the church. Pastors, other paid staff members, and volunteer leaders can always find others to perform many ministry functions far better than they themselves can.

Here's another example from our weekend services. Once the topics and a general outline of the key points of the message have been determined, Mark has no involvement in the planning and preparation of the services with the exception of his message. Other staff and volunteers prepare the stage design, create the media, select the dramas and music, organize the service elements, and make sure everything is rehearsed. When the services take place, all of these efforts have helped to prepare people's hearts to hear the message. By releasing these ministry roles, we're able to accomplish far more during our weekend services than Mark would be able to offer on his own, even though he's gifted in these areas.

In order to do this, Mark has to plan and communicate the topics that he anticipates teaching. This enables others to prepare quality service elements that complement the message and make the teaching more effective.

When you begin to think, "Anything I can do, *you* can do better," the church's leadership capacity is opened up. You'll be able to lead more people, accomplish more tasks, and affect more people's lives. And when this value is shared by others on your team, the church's efforts are multiplied.

—Tony

87

Celebrate in Public and in Private

"Sticks and stones may break my bones, but words will never hurt me."
—*ANONYMOUS LIAR*

I know how to embarrass my oldest daughter. I just tell her what a great job she did on something or how proud I am of her, and she turns six shades of red. I'm convinced that Heather secretly loves to be affirmed, but she often hides her face or tries to change the subject in the face of such affirmation. Of course, as a loving father, that makes me pour it on even more. I want her to know how much I love her and how proud I am of her. When she is sad or lonely or struggling under the weight of life, I want her to remember the words I've spoken to her about her value.

We all have a little "Heather" in us, don't we? We are embarrassed by praise and honor, but oh, how we love to hear it! We may blush at the time, but we reflect on the affirmation for weeks, months, or even years.

I remember when Rob Wegner (another pastor at Granger) spoke some of the most significant words to me that I had ever heard. Soon after we moved into our auditorium, he said, "Tim, I think of this building as your message. I see the quality and attention to detail, and I see your life. I see a man of integrity and values and a man who walks with God." His words marked me.

Words make a difference, don't they? And *when* we say them is important. Sometimes my children need to hear me praise them in front of their siblings or friends. Other times, it's most meaningful when I'm lying beside them on their beds before I pray and kiss them goodnight.

You really can't affirm volunteers too much. Don't succumb to the fear of wondering if you're showing favoritism. The risk of being unfair in your celebration is minimal compared to the repercussions of not developing the practice. Work the habit of affirmation into your schedule so that it comes often and naturally, and think about the time and location that would be most meaningful.

Celebrate in public when...

- you want to use the opportunity to teach others the value of celebration and thanks. At Granger we like to give out "Smooth Stone Awards." We talk about how a volunteer is like the smooth stone that David used to slay the giant. We say, "You have had the same type of impact in your ministry!"
- their sacrifice has gone above and beyond expectations. Their giving has been so remarkable that the entire church (or group) should know.
- their ministry influences a large group of people.

Celebrate in private when...

- you know the individual would be embarrassed by the public spotlight. Some people would rather have their gall bladders removed than be recognized in public.
- you don't want them to question your motives. You want them to know that while this acknowledgment would encourage, educate, and motivate others, this moment is about them. It's all about the contribution of their ministries.
- you want to communicate your praise more personally, in writing. It means a lot to people to receive letters of thanks. They can post them on a mirror, show their closest friends, and keep them forever. Patrick McGoldrick, youth pastor at Cornerstone Baptist Church in Roseville, Michigan, says, "Several times a year I purchase little things for our youth staff. I give the gifts to them while saying thanks for their service."

Contrary to the childhood lie, words *can* wound. But when words are chosen well and spoken in a timely manner, they can add immeasurably to a person's self-esteem and sense of purpose.

—Tim

Track Ministry Connections

"All the Israelites twenty years old or more who were able to serve in
Israel's army were counted according to their families.
The total number was 603,550"
(NUMBERS 1:45-46).

We take time every three months at Granger to complete a
ministry-connections tracking process. Here's how it
works. We send a request to the staff leaders in the church and ask them
each to identify every ministry team in their area, list the members of
that team, and specify who is serving in a leadership role. We collect
these names, enter them into our membership database, and print out
reports summarizing the results. We also compare those numbers to
those of previous periods so we can track increases and decreases in
ministry participation.

With volunteers filling over 2,200 ministry positions at Granger,
you can imagine that this isn't an easy process. We spend many hours
compiling the data and making sure our numbers are accurate. There
are various reasons we've elected to invest this much effort into our
tracking process. Here are a few of them:

Ministry connections measure spiritual maturity. People's
willingness to serve in ministry is one way to monitor steps they are
taking in their faith journeys. People who demonstrate servanthood are
most likely maturing in discipleship.

Tracking connections also confirms ministry health. By
comparing the growth of teams from quarter to quarter, we can monitor whether our ministry connections are keeping pace with the growth
of our church. If ministry connections start to lag, we're reminded that

we need to step up our communications and other systems that help people take steps into ministry.

The data help measure leadership capacity. Do you know whom you can count on to lead in your church? One way is to count the number of people who are following. Additionally, the number of leaders connected in ministry should grow at the same pace as the number of people serving in ministry. Without leadership growth, the ministry will eventually plateau.

Tracking creates a process to identify volunteer gaps. You can quickly learn where certain areas of the ministry need assistance in raising up new volunteers. When you identify those areas, you can focus your communications to help those ministries recruit and connect more people.

Regular collection of data also reminds staff leaders that volunteer team development is a high value. You've probably heard the saying "What gets measured gets done." There's a lot of truth to that statement. If the number of volunteers serving in ministry is always on your radar screen, your staff leaders will be reminded that they have to pay attention to increasing the number of volunteers connected to their ministry areas.

Take the time to regularly count those who are serving on your ministry teams. It will help you discern where the church is healthy and where you need to rally the troops. Volunteers count, so count your volunteers.

—Tony

89

Sometimes You Have to Fire Volunteers

Asking someone *off* the team may be the hardest thing about leadership. These will be some of the most difficult conversations you'll ever have. You'll hear responses that will tear at your heart:

"So I'm not good enough for this church?"

"You think you're better than I am?"

"I've given my life to this church, and now you're telling me that I can no longer participate?"

You will feel deep pain and sometimes significant loss, and yet leadership requires us to make these tough calls.

There are several reasons you might have to "outplace" or "fire" volunteers.

Reasons to Move Them to Someone Else's Team: Sometimes they are in the right position, and they are helping the church, but they should be on someone else's team. It could be because of

- **affinity**—This is merely about chemistry (see Chapter 16, "The Attraction Factor"). There are times when some people on your team don't gel with the other members of the team. It's not sin; it's not right or wrong; it's just affinity. They need to be lovingly placed on another team to which they can better relate.

- **recovery**—Sometimes people should be moved to another team because of the particular phase of life they are passing through. Perhaps they just went through a divorce or the loss of a child, and they just need time to rebuild and recover.

It might help if they are on a team with others who are facing similar hardships or who are in a similar phase of life.

Reasons to Move Them to Different Roles: They might be OK on your team, but they could be in the wrong role due to

- **ability**—They don't have the capacity to do the job, so you need to gently move them to roles in which they can win and the church can win. This issue comes up often in artistic roles that require definite skill levels.

- **availability**—Perhaps they've demonstrated that they can't make the rehearsals or the meetings. It's OK to explain to them that you're moving them to roles with fewer requirements until their schedules change and they are able to recommit to more time-consuming responsibilities.

Reasons to Remove Them From Every Team: Sometimes people should not be serving in the church in any ministry for any reason. The reasons include

- **attitude**—We all struggle with our attitudes from time to time. But if a person continually brings the team down with a bad attitude, you need to address the issue quickly and decisively. Give the person one or two chances to shape up, but realize that eventually you may need to send him or her packing.

> If a person continually brings the team down with a bad attitude, you need to address the issue quickly and decisively.

- **alignment**—Problems with alignment may show up in attitude, fulfillment, or ill-timed questioning. This is a huge issue, which we've addressed more fully in Chapter 62, "Misalignment Is Bad for Tires *and* Churches."

Again, these conversations are never fun. People who say they enjoy tackling these issues are either lying or dysfunctional and in need of a therapist. It always hurts to take action that you know will cause another person pain. So get counsel, pray without ceasing, and remember that our cause is worth being questioned and misunderstood.

—Tim

90

Brand Your Ministries

What comes to mind when you hear the word *Volvo*? Do you think about safety? What about *Nike*? Do images of world-class athletes run through your head? Does your mind immediately jump to Tiger Woods?

Now here's the real test. What comes to mind when you hear the words *Sunday school class*? Be honest. What about *small groups*? Or *junior high ministry*? Yikes! I just had a few scary things run through my mind after that one.

The point I'm making is that, whether you intend to or not, you are fueling the perceptions people have of your church and your ministries. If you want people to think positively of your church and its ministries, you must be intentional about the way you address branding issues. Yes, even ministries need to be concerned with branding.

Branding is the combination of elements such as a name, a logo, or a slogan that identifies and distinguishes a particular product or service and tries to evoke positive perceptions and emotions. In the market-place, branding is used to create a competitive advantage over other goods and services. In our case, branding is used to help people both outside and inside the church understand the ministries and the impact they might have on others' lives. Most churches aren't seeking a competitive advantage over other churches; rather, they're trying to position themselves to influence people in a culture that is constantly trying to grab and keep people's attention and loyalties.

If your church is intentional about reaching the unchurched, you should be particularly attuned to the importance of branding. Your community is living in a culture saturated with slick marketing campaigns. People's expectations and perceptions of credibility are being influenced by how the marketplace delivers its message. The unchurched are more likely to question the credibility of the church's message if it is unprofessional, inconsistent, and lacking creativity. And since we're offering the most important message in the world, shouldn't we be concerned about that?

Fellowship Church (www.fellowshipchurch.com) in Grapevine, Texas, understands the importance of branding. Just visit their Web site to get an amazing lesson on the power of positioning your message in today's culture. Here's what you might notice as you check out the brands of Fellowship Church:

Simplicity—The brands they've chosen are simple and easy to remember. Take, for example, Surge, their junior high ministry. Isn't that cool? The images that spring to mind of a weekly "surge" are very different from the images of a "gathering for junior high students on Sunday morning."

Visual Appeal—The brand isn't just the name, it's the way the name is visually presented. The graphics help communicate the culture and the values of the ministry.

Creative Approach—If you use a standard name to define your ministries, then you also get the baggage many people carry from previous church experiences. "Small groups" is an example. Although your small groups may be great, newcomers may have had negative experiences in small groups. Fellowship Church uses the term *HomeTeams* to describe small groups, which allows them to start fresh in communicating that ministry to their target.

Creating quality brands within your church not only helps to attract new people who are served by those ministries, but it also helps with recruiting volunteers. For the longest time, we had difficulty attracting people to serve on our greeter team, on our ushering crew, at our information center, and in several other roles that affect our

guests' first experiences at Granger. So several years ago, we began branding those ministries with the name *First Impressions*. That helped us better communicate the purpose and value of the ministry, and more people wanted to be a part of the team that was making quality "first impressions" at Granger.

> Focus your branding efforts on the highest priority ministries first.

Here's a word of caution as you are developing your branding strategy. Your highest ministry priorities should get the best quality names, slogans, and graphics. Just because you have talented marketing and artistic people serving in small-group ministry, for example, doesn't mean that the ministry should have a slick logo while your church logo remains dated. The way in which the message is communicated should reflect the scope of the overall mission and vision of the church. Focus your branding efforts on the highest priority ministries first.

Make sure you're paying attention to your church's branding strategies, and confirm that they're creating the perceptions you want people to have of your ministry. If you haven't thought about it recently, well, it's time to "just do it."

—Tony

91

Sometimes the Church Messes Up

Mr. Smith (not his real name) had attended our church for about five years with his family. He loved the church and grew spiritually with his wife. When she got sick a few months ago, he was heartbroken. Members of our hospital visitation team visited both of them in the hospital a few times, but when it was clear she wouldn't make it, Mr. Smith requested a visit from a pastor. A series of foul-ups followed:

Mistake 1: The message was never communicated, and his wife died before any pastor visited.

Mistake 2: Again because of miscommunication, no pastor attended or was involved in his wife's funeral.

Mistake 3: One of our pastors sent a letter apologizing for our error, and offered condolences for his loss. However, the letter was inadvertently addressed to both *Mr. and Mrs. Smith* and said that we were sorry for the passing of his mother (who is still very much alive).

Mistake 4: The next piece of correspondence he received from the church was an update on the monetary pledge he and his wife had made a couple of years ago. It was perceived as a "past due notice" and was addressed to both him and his wife.

Mistake 5: As he expressed his frustration on the phone to one of our staff members, she assured him that we would make the appropriate corrections. She inadvertently closed the conversation by saying, "Now tell me again your wife's name."

After all of these foul-ups, Mr. Smith was understandably convinced that no one at the church cared about him or his family. He believed that we were a big church and he was just a number. He felt as if no one cared about him or his pain. We were so far "in the hole" with Mr. Smith that there would probably never be a way to make it right.

Sometimes the church messes up in big ways. This happens with staff members, and it happens with volunteers. Anytime humans and human-made systems are in place, mistakes will happen. The church exists to help and heal, not to cause pain. So it is always painful when a mistake you make causes pain in anyone's life, especially when you know, in hindsight, that it could have been avoided.

Here are some things to remember when a staff or volunteer leader at your church messes up:

Don't make excuses. If it was a mistake, acknowledge it. It doesn't matter that we were in the midst of a database migration to new software and a few things fell through the cracks during the transition. The folks who have been hurt don't care. It doesn't matter. Your excuses won't help to minimize their pain. Just shoot straight: "I am so sorry for the pain we caused you. We were very wrong. Will you please forgive us?"

Stand with your team. If someone on your team or in your church is the one who made the mistake, don't apologize for "his" or "her" mistake. Use the word *we* or *I* when referring to the screw-up. "*I* am very sorry." "*We* messed up." "*We* made a mistake." Stand with your team.

Sometimes their pain will heal only through separation. There are some things you can't fix. Mr. Smith will probably never attend our church again. Don't focus on that individual's image of your church. It's already been ruined, and you can't fix it. Instead, focus on his soul. Focus on his growth. As you talk to him, communicate your care for him: "I know that you may never want to attend our church again. But please don't give up on God. Please find a place where you can worship and heal this deep wound."

Always make changes after making mistakes. As a leader, you must make changes after mistakes are made. If you continue to see similar mistakes being made again and again, then you haven't learned anything. The only way to redeem a screw-up is to make sure it doesn't happen again. Change systems or leaders or processes, but always follow through every time to ensure you don't do it again.

Mr. Smith is precious to God, and we are determined to never let the pain we caused him happen to anyone else in our church.

—Tim

It's True...
Relationships
Change Lives

"I can't imagine anything more enjoyable than being with a group of friends to work at expanding God's kingdom while at the same time laughing, telling stories, and experiencing life together."

—*TED HAGGARD*[1]

We are all children at heart, aren't we? I mean, anytime someone says, "Sign up for the hayride" or "Attend a leadership conference" or "Come work in the nursery," one of our first questions is always "Who else is going?" We don't want to commit, contribute, or invest our time until we have the answer to "Who else?" Why? Because we all want to hang around people we like.

My introduction to ministry began as an eighth-grader. Darrell, Becky, Pennie, Jana, and I were responsible for Bus 2 at our church. Every Saturday we would drive the streets of inner-city Des Moines for five hours and visit every child on our bus route. We would shower them with love and remind them that we would pick them up for church on Sunday morning. Then when Sunday came, we would pack the bus with seventy or eighty kids and take them to church. We would sing songs and tell stories all the way there and spend time listening and loving on the way home.

I loved it! Was it because I had an affinity with kids? Partially. Was it because we were sharing the gospel message with kids who hadn't heard it? That was pretty cool. But mostly I just loved living life with my friends while making a difference in our world. We laughed, told stories, argued, prayed, challenged one another, and wept together. And when, after a few years, Becky was killed in a car accident, we became even closer. Two days after her death, we visited each child to share the news and give each one a hug. We were determined to carry on Becky's ministry.

Those relationships changed my life. They made me a better person. They planted within me a desire to have an impact on my world. They convinced me that life has purpose and meaning when we are experiencing it with people we love.

Relationships change lives. As a church leader, you must believe this. You must believe to your core that people who are in relationships with others in your church are more likely to grow. They are more likely to take steps in their faith. They are more likely to invite their friends to church. They are more likely to share their faith and give their time and invest their money. Relationships change lives!

> You must believe to your core that people who are in relationships with others in your church are more likely to grow.

If you truly believe this, it will affect the way you do church. It will influence your priorities! It will alter how you preach and what you say. It will also change the way you invite people into ministry. Remember, you are not asking them to fill a spot. You are not asking them to do a task or complete a job. You are inviting them into life-transforming relationships! You are giving them an opportunity that has the potential to change their lives forever!

—Tim

ENDNOTE

1. Ted Haggard, *Dog Training, Fly Fishing, and Sharing Christ in the 21st Century* (Nashville, TN: Thomas Nelson, Inc., 2002), 9.

93

Find Your Focus

Tim and I recently sat down for dinner with a pastor from a church much larger than Granger. Like pastors of most growing churches, we're constantly seeking advice from those who are a few steps ahead of us to determine what we need to do to remove barriers to additional growth. One of the questions we ask is "What are the most important things we need to consider to continue reaching more people for Jesus?" Or in our case, "What will we need to do differently as a church of ten thousand from what we currently do as a church of five thousand?"

The answer we received may surprise you. He told us, "Always figure out what you're *not* going to do." This pastor recommended that we continue to focus our ministry on the priorities. He encouraged us to figure out how God has best positioned our church for ministry and then to concentrate our resources in those areas. He suggested that we mustn't be afraid to cut ministry programs as the church grows. We need to keep the main thing the main thing.

Now wouldn't you have expected the opposite of a growing church? Wouldn't you

> Keep the main thing the main thing.

expect to see a church with attendance exceeding ten thousand people each weekend to be *adding* ministry programming rather than cutting it?

When churches lose sight of this important principle, they begin to lose the laser focus on their vision. When everyone isn't completely focused on the main thing, other messages end up getting the attention. When announcement time comes around in the service, newcomers hear the important stuff, but they also hear about programs or events that aren't really the highest priority. When churches lack focus, their communications begin to blur and they aren't as effective. The sermons, the platform announcements, the bulletin, the newsletter, and the Web sites should all clearly point to the main thing.

Resource challenges are another indication of the need to refocus. When new ministry programs continue to be added, a church is left with reductions in leaders, staff, money, facility space, and volunteers for existing ministry programs. It's simple math. Let's assume a church has one hundred volunteers and $10,000 to spend. When it adds only one new ministry program, a portion of those volunteers and some of that money are going to be diverted. This, quite obviously, leaves fewer volunteers and financial resources for the existing ministries.

> Churches that don't proactively rein in the programming will continue to find it difficult to recruit enough volunteers.

Additionally, the resource challenges don't go away as the church grows. In fact, our experience at Granger is that the resource issues are magnified because it takes many more volunteers and dollars to provide the same level of programming as the church grows.

I hear leaders in other churches complain from time to time about difficulties in finding volunteers for their children's ministry, for example. Then I look at the church calendar and see the number of programs and events they're trying to pull off. It's astounding that they can find any volunteers at all because people are overwhelmed with requests to help out in multiple ministries and are asked to attend growing numbers of ministry events. Churches that don't proactively rein in the programming will continue to find it difficult to recruit enough volunteers.

This principle is true in families, in relationships, in businesses, and in churches. The more you focus your attention and resources, the better results you'll experience. If you focus your time and attention on just a few friendships, you'll develop deep relationships. If you try to maintain hundreds of friendships, you'll end up with hundreds of acquaintances. The same holds true for ministry. That's why it's so important to find and maintain your focus.

—Tony

94

Empowerment Is More Than Delegation

"He appointed twelve—designating them apostles—
that they might be with him and that he might send them out to
preach and to have authority to drive out demons"
(MARK 3:14-15).

There's a difference between giving a volunteer a task to complete and empowering someone to carry on ministry. One has the potential to add more to your workload in the long run; the other releases the potential for ministry growth. As we discuss in Chapter 55, "Not All Volunteers Are Created Equal," some people are "doers." They either don't desire or don't have the capacity for further leadership roles. Others, however, can take ownership of key ministry functions; in those instances you need to give away more than just the task.

Jesus modeled empowerment when he selected the twelve apostles who would carry on ministry after he returned to heaven. Here's how he approached this transition:

First, he trained them *("...that they might be with him...")*. Jesus spent time with his appointed team, equipping them for future ministry. He didn't just launch them into specific roles. He prepared them for the challenges they would face by inviting them to hang out with him and learn from his teachings and interactions with others.

Next, he sent them to train and recruit others *("...send them out to preach...")*. He encouraged them to continue reaching more people by sharing the good news and preparing others for ministry. Jesus wanted them to teach and train others who could carry on the ministry once he returned to heaven (see also 2 Timothy 2:2).

Finally, he empowered them to care for others *("...have authority to drive out demons.")*. Jesus didn't just give the teaching ministry away; he also asked the apostles to provide care for the people they were trying to reach. Sometimes in our churches, we don't set up our lay leaders to move beyond the shepherding and teaching roles to the point where people not only accept but expect volunteer leaders to provide care and counsel when crises come along. Instead of going to their small-group leader, a Sunday school teacher, or a ministry team leader, people go to their pastors as the first line of defense. When the paid professional is the *only* person who can handle that ministry responsibility, church growth plateaus.

If you really want to empower volunteers, give them more than a task. Give them ownership of their ministry roles. Define the outcomes you desire, and give them the freedom to determine the methods and strategies to fulfill those objectives. This strategic shift in how you position volunteers will help your church move beyond incremental growth so that you can reach and care for more and more people.

—Tony

95

Tap Painful Experiences

"But God chose the foolish things of the world to shame the wise;
God chose the weak things of the world to shame the strong"
(1 CORINTHIANS 1:27).

We all have baggage. For some of us, it is dysfunctional family baggage. For others it's religious baggage. Some of us were victims and have deep wounds inflicted by others. Some carry the baggage of self-inflicted pain due to bad choices or lifestyles. Even the most sheltered person who grew up in a Christian home has baggage (sometimes called sheltered-Christian-home baggage).

We all carry our baggage differently. Some people put their baggage on display so that it's visible a hundred yards away. Their lives are defined by their baggage. They talk about it, ask for prayer about it, complain about it, and use it as an excuse for everything that's wrong in their lives.

Others are ashamed. They don't want anyone to know. Their baggage affects them more than they know. They aren't even sure whether *God* can love them, so they are confident they'd be scorned and humiliated if any human found out.

Some have dealt with their baggage and seem rather stable. However, when you get to know them, you discover that they've faced some pretty heavy stuff and they have amazing stories about the redemption of God.

> God never wastes an experience, no matter how horrific.

Everyone has baggage. The great thing, though, is that God is the best "baggage handler." He pours out his grace on those who have been wronged, and he forgives those who have sinned. God never wastes an experience, no matter how horrific.

Everyone on your team has a story. If you look deep enough into the eyes of the precious people around you, you'll see the pain that they carry. You'll see the mistakes they've made and the wounds that are still healing. The good news is that God can use their stories. If they'll let him, he can tap their pain and use it to help others.

As a leader, it's your job to help your volunteers continue the healing process. Help them to see what God sees when he looks at them. Help them to use their hurt to help others whose scars are even fresher than their own.

I love the way that *The Message* paraphrases the reminder from Paul to the Corinthians: "Take a good look, friends, at who you were when you got called into this life. I don't see many of 'the brightest and the best' among you, not many influential, not many from high-society families. Isn't it obvious that God deliberately chose men and women that the culture overlooks and exploits and abuses, chose these 'nobodies' to expose the hollow pretensions of the 'somebodies'? That makes it quite clear that none of you can get by with blowing your own horn before God. Everything that we have—right thinking and right living, a clean slate and a fresh start—comes from God by way of Jesus Christ. That's why we have the saying, 'If you're going to blow a horn, blow a trumpet for God' " (1 Corinthians 1:26-31, *The Message*).

It's a good reminder. We're all human. We've all messed up, and we all need help. You've heard the phrase "Hurt people hurt people." In the church, let's change that to "Hurt people help other hurting people heal."

—Tim

96

Add Fun People to the Team

"I have told you this so that you will be filled with my joy.
Yes, your joy will overflow!"
(JOHN 15:11, NLT).

Where is the joy? Jesus has given you new life. You have received forgiveness for all your sins—past, present, and future. You have purpose. You have hope. You've experienced amazing grace. Your home in heaven is waiting. You are a new creation. You have the power of the Holy Spirit working on your behalf. You are victorious. You've been delivered from Satan's domain. Christ is living inside you. You've been declared righteous. You're a child of God. You are accepted, you are protected, and you are loved. So I ask you, "Where is the joy?"

Your attitude is your decision. As a leader, the attitudes of those on your team are also *your* decision. You should expect people to be happy. Happy people attract more happy people. If you want to experience church growth, you should be ever conscious of the attitude of your congregation. If there is no joy in Mudville, there will be no people in your pews.

As followers of Christ, we should be experiencing joy. The joy should be overflowing in our lives. That attitude should be a reflection of our faith in Jesus. It should be a reflection

> You should expect people to be happy.

of the fruit of the Spirit in our lives. It's also a reflection of a decision we can make each day to choose joy over sadness or anger or bitterness.

As our kids have grown up, we've tried to impart this basic principle to them. There are appropriate times for sadness and anger, but most times, particularly as toddlers, our kids have needed to learn to choose joy. That's why, when they were emotionally spent and in the middle of a tantrum, we've sent them to another place in the house so they wouldn't interrupt everyone else's joy.

Our younger daughter, Abby, has been a little bit more expressive in this area than our first two kids. Because of that, she's spent quite a bit of time in her room considering "the opportunity" to be joyful. After she learned to talk, the routine would look something like this. She would throw a tantrum and start screaming and crying. We would take her up to her room. We wouldn't even close the door. All we would say is "You can come downstairs when you decide to be happy." After a while, we'd hear her footsteps as she descended the stairs, and then she would enter the room and announce, "I'm happy now." Abby has learned that happiness is a choice.

> Emotions are
> a choice.

It's important for adults also to understand that their emotions are a choice. As a pastor or ministry leader, you hold people accountable for moral integrity. You hold them accountable for growing in their faith journeys. You hold them accountable for their performances in ministry. It's just as important that you hold them accountable for their attitudes.

This principle is particularly important when you're selecting people who will be close to you in leadership. Whether they're paid staff assistants or lay leaders, their attitudes should count. You should find people with whom you enjoy spending time. Add fun people to your team. As you do that over time, you'll find that the entire atmosphere of your ministry will change. No more morale problems, no more negative vibes. Believe it or not, even churches can be happy places!

Now look around you. Do you see people expressing joy? If not, it may be time to send them to their rooms and tell them, "You can come out when you decide to be happy."

—Tony

Helping High-Capacity People

97

Out of every fifty volunteers, one or two will have a high capacity for achievement. They have huge gifts and skills in several different areas. They are committed to the vision of the church, and they want to give as much time as they can to the mission. They have varying passions and interests, and they have the discretionary time to give to three or more ministry areas.

For these individuals, it's not a question of *if* they will serve. It's not a matter of finding the right ministries. For them, there might be ten different ministry positions in which they could make a huge difference. Your job is to help them find the areas in which they'll have the greatest impact.

Recently my friend Jeff came to me with this dilemma. He was involved in eight significant ministry areas, and it was becoming apparent to him and his family that he needed to focus. Rather than doing OK in some of these areas, he wanted to stay only in those ministries in which he had the time and energy to "hit the ball out of the park."

The problem with Jeff is that he is highly gifted. God blessed him with more skills than most of us mortals, and he has a lot of interests and abilities. So he went through an exercise that I think could be reproduced and used by others:

Put everything on paper. Jeff began by writing down all of his ministry involvements. He listed everything that took a notable amount of time. Even within high school ministry, where he has served for years, he listed two separate responsibilities that each take a huge block of time. He ended up with eight significant areas of ministry on his list.

Organize according to your SHAPE. Jeff then began writing letters by each ministry. Using the SHAPE acronym that Tony described in Chapter 21, "Learn How People Are Wired," he put an S by each area in which he believed he had a God-given spiritual gift. He placed an H by each area in which his heart was engaged. He placed an A next to each responsibility in which he exercised abilities and skills. He believed his personality fit well in some ministries; next to them, he jotted a P. He placed an E beside those that matched his life experiences.

When he'd finished, he had three or four letters beside some ministries and only one letter beside others.

Get counsel from those you trust. Then he took one more step. He began to meet with some of those ministry leaders and others who know him well, and he asked where he had the greatest impact. "Where can I be most effective?" "What are the things I do that give the church the biggest return?" He asked them to be straight with him. He really wanted to know.

Adjust and focus. Then he made changes based on that feedback. It took some maturity, since he enjoyed all eight areas and didn't want to give anything up. But he prayed, thought, listened, analyzed, and then acted. Jeff knows that he'll be more effective, in the long run, by focusing on a few things.

This is a great process. Share it with the high-capacity people in your church. You might find that your effectiveness as a church will increase, rather than decrease, when everyone gets focused.

—Tim

98

Avoid the Blame Game

I'm sure this doesn't happen in your church, but maybe you've heard about it happening in other churches. The staff and existing lay leaders get frustrated because they're overburdened with ministry responsibilities, while a number of people who could help out are sitting on the sidelines. The leaders begin complaining about the fact that people aren't stepping up to volunteer. The tendency is to blame the people who haven't committed to ministry. *They* are the problem.

In most cases, however, I think situations like these are less often people problems and more often leadership or systems problems. Rather than pinning the blame for a lack of volunteers on those who aren't serving, I suggest the problem may be better addressed by answering the following questions:

Is it a vision problem? Have you defined and regularly communicated a clear vision that people are willing to support with their spiritual gifts, time, and financial resources? If not, you may need to redefine your vision.

Is it a communications problem? Have you effectively communicated the opportunities to serve throughout the ministry? Do people know that one of the core values of your church is to serve on a ministry team with other Christ-followers?

Is it a leadership problem? Are you modeling well by connecting in relationships with people and helping them take steps in their faith journeys? Are you helping to disciple those under your direct influence so that they are learning to become good stewards of their resources and abilities? Are you actively encouraging others to connect in ministry?

Is it a focus problem? Is your church trying to do too much? I can tell you from my experience in consulting with a number of local churches that a common temptation is to try to pull off too much ministry programming. When you try to do too much, you spread your resources, including your volunteers, too thinly across the entire ministry. The most effective ministries maintain a laser focus on their mission and vision, and they ruthlessly eliminate anything that doesn't fit that strategy.

Is it a systems problem? Do people know how to connect with a ministry team? Is there a way for them to discover their gift mix and learn how their passions might best fit the church's current ministries? When someone calls the office and wants to help out, does someone from your leadership team immediately respond, providing more information and identifying for that person the next steps to connect in ministry?

Is it a spiritual maturity issue? Even if it is, you and your existing leaders are accountable to God for the spiritual development of those in your church. You can help them fall deeply in love with Jesus so they capture the passion for fulfilling the Great Commandment and the Great Commission that you have.

Don't allow the leaders around you to slip into the blame game when people aren't volunteering to help out in ministry. In addition to promoting a negative environment that in itself isn't very attractive to others, you're not helping your team proactively address the issues that are more likely to be keeping people on the sidelines. Don't let your team slip into victim mode. Instead, sit down with your leadership team and have a heart-to-heart dialogue beginning with the questions outlined in this chapter. You may be surprised by the way a few simple changes can dramatically affect how receptive people are to jumping into the game and starting to serve.

—Tony

Don't Give Up

People will leave your church.

People will call you names and stab you in the back.

People will stomp on your dreams and laugh at your ambition. They will spotlight your failures and minimize your successes. They will suck the life out of you when they have a need, and they will kick the life out of you when you feel weak.

As the pressure of ministry increases, you will be tempted to throw in the towel. You will want to let down your guard and give someone a piece of your mind. You will want to cut corners and make compromises. You will sometimes be curled up in a corner, not even confident that you have enough strength to walk across the room.

You will read books like this one and be frustrated by the concise, short chapters. "My problems can't be solved in five hundred words or less," you'll say. You'll hear about the visible success of other churches, and you'll smile on the outside but groan on the inside. The thoughts that you could never voice seem to be in the forefront of your mind: "Why is God blessing their efforts and not mine? Why does God seem to be smiling on every other church and frowning on my ministry?"

You hear about the growth of another church or the "miracle gift" it just received from an anonymous millionaire, and you say the right words ("Praise God! I'm so happy for you"), but in fact, you really just want to give up: "Let others lead this ministry…maybe they could make some progress."

No matter how stable your personality is, whether you are an introvert or extrovert, pessimist or optimist, you have faced times when you've wanted to give up. Me too. Sometimes we just want to quit. We are sick and tired of people and problems, and we are tired of explaining ourselves at every turn. If we are honest with ourselves, sometimes we want to take the advice of Job's wife: "Are you still holding on to your integrity? Curse God and die!" (Job 2:9).

There are times when moving to a new ministry or a different church would be exactly the right decision. But so often, we just give up too soon.

"When people ask me about how Granger has continued to grow," says Mark Beeson, who founded the church in 1986, "I tell them I just didn't give up. Day after day, week after week, year after year, I just kept taking the next step and was determined not to give up." I'm convinced that one of the major differences between growing churches and those that are not growing is that the leaders of growing churches just keep going. They push through the troubles, turmoil, and conflict and refuse to give up.

> Leaders of growing churches just keep going. They push through the troubles, turmoil, and conflict and refuse to give up.

And it doesn't get any easier as you grow. Mark often recounts a conference he attended several years ago in which a pastor of one of the largest churches in America at that time said that pastoring a large church was much easier than pastoring a small church. "I have time to write and travel more than ever before. You pastors [of smaller churches] have a much harder job than I have," the speaker remarked.

Now as Granger exceeds five thousand in attendance many weekends, Mark is convinced that this man was lying. "Ministry has never been harder in my life, and the pressure has never been greater," he says. "I keep waiting for it to get easier, but the weight of the ministry grows exponentially each year."

You are not alone in your feelings. The great theologian (I'm kidding, of course) Ross Perot said, "Most people give up just when they're about to achieve success. They quit on the one-yard line. They give up at the last minute of the game, one foot from a winning touchdown." This is true in the church as well.

When your actions are questioned, don't give up.

When you are unfairly attacked, don't give up.

When you make mistakes and can't seem to get anything right, don't give up.

When the schedule is unbearable, and you're not sure you can take one more step, don't give up.

When you feel as if you can't do anything to please anyone, don't give up.

When it seems as if the only person who likes you is your spouse (and even he or she wavers at times), don't give up.

When you've just been betrayed by your best friend who you thought would never leave your side, don't give up.

When there are so many demands on you that you don't think you can stand under the weight, don't give up.

When you are preparing your message and you are so empty that you can't find anything to say, don't give up.

When the air is thick and the clouds are dense and you can't see far enough ahead of you to know if you are going in the right direction, don't give up.

Just take your next step. Do the next right thing. Don't try to figure out next week or next year; just put one foot in front of the other and concentrate on your next step. God will give you grace and strength to get to the other side.

> "Let us not become weary in doing good,
> for at the proper time we will reap a
> harvest if we do not give up"
> *(GALATIANS 6:9).*

—Tim

Discussion Guide

One helpful way to use this book is to read it with your team. You may want to consider reading ten chapters every week for the next ten weeks. Schedule an hour to come together to discuss what you've learned, and map out a plan for ministry improvements. Here are some questions to help guide your discussion:

1. In the chapters you read this week, what idea most challenged your thinking?

2. Of the principles that were covered, do you consider any to be inaccurate or inappropriate for your ministry environment?

3. Are there any obvious or easy changes that would improve the ministry effectiveness of your church? If so, what are they? Is there anything preventing you from implementing them immediately?

4. What insight would involve the most risk for implementation but could offer the biggest reward? Do you believe God is calling you to take that risk?

5. What is the most pressing question you're left with from the topics covered? Where do you need discernment or further study to know if it's a change God really wants for your church?

6. Has this week's reading caused you to consider anything in your personal leadership approach that you would like to change?

7. What action step could your ministry team take to improve the effectiveness of your church's ministry? Who will be responsible for that action step? What is your target date for implementation?

Topical Index

Announcements 123
Attitude 73, 208, 223
Authenticity 147, 185
Balance 75, 89, 143
Branding 210
Calling 151, 163, 195
Capacity 107, 134, 167, 169, 176, 195, 206, 219, 225
Care 45, 132
Change .213
Chunking 21
Commissioning 138
Communication . . . 17, 32, 41, 61, 65, 67, 77, 87, 105, 123, 125, 145, 178, 187, 191, 210, 227
Conflict . .32, 36, 61, 77, 87, 89, 91, 116, 127, 145, 160, 178
Connections 165
Creativity 93, 210
Culture . .19, 28, 55, 63, 65, 67, 73, 119, 121, 193
Decision making 116
Discipline . . 91, 113, 149, 178, 208
Empowerment . . 53, 57, 69, 85, 96, 147, 165, 201, 219
Encouragement 26, 32, 61, 77, 93, 111, 167, 171, 178, 181, 204
Evaluation 189, 206
Events 63, 69, 187, 189, 197
Failure 93, 213, 221
Family 39
First impressions 121, 158
Focus 73, 217, 225, 227
Growth 65, 156, 217
Leadership . . 30, 34, 47, 49, 51, 53, 85, 87, 93, 100, 102, 113, 116, 138, 143, 169, 201, 227, 229

Legacy .151
Legalism 153
Measurements 125, 153
Meetings 89, 116, 191
Mentoring 167
Ministry roles . .19, 21, 41, 43, 130, 134, 163
Obedience 80
Outreach 75, 109, 143, 153
Prayer 167, 191
Preparation 187
Relationships 215
Selling .160
Span of care 55, 71, 130, 225
Spiritual gifts . . .19, 59, 107, 134, 147, 225
Spiritual maturity . . .75, 80, 109, 113, 153, 176, 206, 227
Staffing . .23, 65, 102, 134, 169, 185
Storytelling 119, 183, 221
Structure 21, 34, 71, 130, 136
Surveys 125
Systems 82, 98, 100, 125, 140, 156, 171, 189, 206, 227
Team building . .17, 21, 36, 39, 41, 45, 55, 57, 63, 69, 80, 96, 100, 107, 109, 123, 145, 156, 163, 174, 197
Titles 85
Training 32, 53, 132, 158, 163, 167, 176, 178, 199, 219
Unity 116, 140, 149, 191, 208
Vision 17, 23, 47, 49, 55, 102, 140, 187, 217, 227
Voting .116
Web care 43, 169
Worship 30, 153

About the Authors

Tony Morgan is the pastor of administrative services at Granger Community Church (www.gccwired.com). After receiving a bachelor's degree in Business Administration and a master's in Public Administration from Bowling Green State University in Ohio, Tony spent almost ten years serving in local government—most recently in Niles, Michigan, as city administrator. As the chief executive officer of this community, he had responsibility for over 150 employees and a $20 million budget. He transitioned into church leadership in 1998 and now helps lead one of the fastest growing churches in the country. He serves on the senior management team at Granger where he contributes as a strategic thinker and practical visionary. Tony has written numerous articles on staffing, technology, strategic planning, and other church leadership topics.

Tim Stevens is the executive pastor at Granger, where he has served for over a decade. After nine years in leadership with Life Action Ministries, Tim joined Granger in 1994 when there were four hundred people attending and five staff members. As executive pastor, he has helped the church grow to over five thousand in weekly attendance with a staff of over fifty. He has overseen five major construction projects, dozens of staff hires, and the development of the church's vision and values, branding, and strategic plan for the future. Tim led the completion of Granger's new interactive children's center, which has been featured in numerous publications for its innovative approach to reaching families.

In addition to their roles at Granger, Tony and Tim desire to resource other ministries. Together, they launched WiredChurches.com, Granger's ministry to church leaders around the world. They have presented workshops to several thousand leaders and have trained churches through conferences and consulting. In addition to *Simply Strategic Volunteers*, Tony and Tim co-authored the first book in this series, *Simply Strategic Stuff: Help for Leaders Drowning in the Details of Running a Church* (Group Publishing, 2004).

Additional Resources

This book was written to help pastors and other leaders implement ministry infrastructure that encourages spiritual and church growth. Many other resources intended for this purpose are available through WiredChurches.com, a ministry of Granger Community Church in Granger, Indiana.

Over the past several years, church staff and volunteer leaders have frequented WiredChurches.com and training events hosted on the Granger campus to learn more about the church's ministry strategy. Here are a number of ways WiredChurches.com is prepared to train and equip you and your team:

Innovative Church Conference

The Innovative Church Conference is offered each year to provide cutting-edge communications, media, and leadership principles for the church. Learn from the recent experiences of the Granger team, and hear from some of the leading voices in American churches today. This conference will provide your team with the latest thoughts and trends in our culture and the church. Together we will learn, we will dream, and we will be inspired.

Simply Strategic Workshops

Tim and Tony host a one-day workshop several times during the year to dig more deeply into the concepts offered in their books, *Simply Strategic Stuff* and *Simply Strategic Volunteers*. Spend time with them on the Granger campus (or ask about hosting a workshop at your location), and see firsthand how these principles have been implemented. These highly interactive workshops will give you a chance to ask questions about how the principles apply to your ministry setting.

WiredChurches.com Workshops

In addition to the Simply Strategic workshop, Granger's staff leaders present several other seminars throughout the year on specific ministry topics such as creative arts, facilities management, small groups, and first impressions.

WiredChurches.com Resources

WiredChurches.com provides many useful resources for church leaders including message subscriptions, graphic downloads, media samples, and music. For ordering information, call 1-888-249-6480, or visit www.wiredchurches.com.

Consulting and Speaking

WiredChurches.com is your connection to personalized consulting, training, and speaking opportunities offered by the key leaders of Granger Community Church. Contact WiredChurches.com to tap into expert advice on topics such as strategic planning, organizational development, construction planning, first impressions, missions outreach, children's ministry, student ministry, and creative arts.

WiredChurches.com Web Site

WiredChurches.com has the most current information available about conferences, workshops, new leadership resources, and insights into the ministry of Granger Community Church. Log on today to learn more and to subscribe to our free e-newsletter.

WiredChurches
630 E. University Drive
Granger, IN 46530
Phone: (888) 249-6480
Fax: (574) 243-3510
Web: www.wiredchurches.com

wiredChurches.com

Also in the Simply Strategic Series...

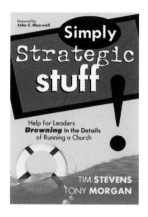

Simply Strategic Stuff

Help for Leaders Drowning in the
Details of Running a Church
with foreword by John C. Maxwell

"This is an excellent administrative book for purpose-driven pastors...We highly recommend the PDC-friendly book, *Simply Strategic Stuff*."
—Five stars from Rick Warren's *Ministry Toolbox*, www.pastors.com

"It's easy to become so consumed with doing church that we don't slow down long enough to evaluate what we're doing. Tim and Tony have done some thinking for us all. *Simply Strategic Stuff* is full of innovative ideas to help you programmatically and strategically."
—Andy Stanley, Senior Pastor, North Point Community Church

"A map of the emerging church that does not include this book is not worth a glance. You may not agree with all ninety-nine strategies—I didn't—but ninety-eight out of ninety-nine ain't bad."
—Leonard Sweet, Drew Theological School, preachingplus.com

Simply Strategic Stuff
ISBN 0-7644-2625-7
(Group Publishing, Inc., 2004)
To order, go to www.simplystrategicstuff.com. Or order from your favorite Christian book supplier, purchase online at www.group.com, or contact Group Publishing, P.O. Box 485, Loveland, CO 80539-0485.

Look for Tim and Tony's third book in the Simply Strategic Series, *Simply Strategic Growth*, available June 2005!